ECCENTRICITY AND BEYOND

John Spencer

ASHRIDGE PRESS

Published and distributed by
Ashridge Press
A subsidiary of Country Books

ISBN 1 901214 03 6

*Whilst some of the happenings contained within these stories reflect real
events, the names of the people involved have been changed to protect their
confidentiality. Many of them have since died, but alive or dead, I wish to
thank them all for unwittingly contributing to the richness and variety of
my medical experiences over the last thirty years.*

Design, typesetting and production:
Country Books, Little Longstone,
Bakewell, Derbyshire DE45 1NN

Tel/Fax: 01629 640670
e-mail: dickrichardson@country-books.co.uk

Printed and bound by: Antony Rowe Ltd, Chippenham, Wiltshire

ECCENTRICITY

1 .The quality of being abnormally centred; of not being con-
centric; of not having the axis in the centre.

2.The quality or habit of deviating from what is customary,
irregularity, oddity, whimsicality.

August 2014
Thanks for a very
enjoyable four week
back in Great Longstone

John, Pat and Matthew .

CONTENTS

INTRODUCTION

The psychiatrist can be socially disadvantaged, sometimes to the point of ostracism and at the most urbane and light hearted gatherings one fears being asked what one does for a living. The lawyer, the green grocer or the teacher are usually accepted for being what they are if they answer truthfully. Not so the honest psychiatrist! On admitting to ones chosen profession there is usually a short silence, a palpable stiffening and a veil of unease descends, followed by a change in tone of voice, facial expression and a defensive posture in the inquirer. Occasionally hostility and distrust are experienced whilst others display a sort of narcissistic curiosity or awe. At other times inquiries are made as to whether you are able to deduce the contents of the mind of the other or perhaps analyze on the spot the hidden meaning underlying the others every utterance and gesture. "Could I tell you about this interesting dream I keep having?" or "what do you think about Bill Clinton?" are typical of the sort of inane questions which make you wish you that you had stayed home or gone to see a movie.

On some occasions the inquirer sees the meeting as an opportunity to discuss problems they are having with a relative or neighbour currently receiving counselling for agoraphobia or a friends daughter with anorexia. Sometimes the partygoer will express irritation and negative feelings to the hapless shrink or to the psychiatric profession as a whole.

There are various strategies for dealing with this uninvited form of social stigmatization.These range from lying about ones job (I have a colleague who tells everyone he is a musician) or simply staying at home.Other friends avoid the term completely and refer to themselves as physicians in behavioural medicine, mental health specialists or behavioural neurologists. Whilst some of these attitudes reflect ignorance, misunderstanding and prejudice towards the mentally ill it is probably true that psychiatrists themselves are partly to blame for as a sub group of the human species they have been trained to listen, observe and diagnose the inner world of others mental processing. Whether or not they do this effectively and efficiently is not the point as unwittingly they have developed the complex habit of scrutinizing others in a similar manner that the artist is unable to refrain from studying a painting on the waiting room wall or the musician commenting on piped music in a restaurant.

The psychiatrist shares with other mental health workers, lawyers, the clergy, and those who work in prison and parole systems a unique and in some ways privileged window into some of the more unusual, sometimes disagreeable,often absurd, and at times bizarre manifestations of the human condition. Whilst most of the population seek intrigue and entertainment from an inexhaustible litany of television thrillers, contemporary novels and videos, for this group of professionals there is nothing on the screen or printed page that they have not witnessed during the proceedings of the last working week. The bizarre, the odd, the eccentric and the unbelievably extra-ordinary stories which are mass produced for public entertainment are all familiar territory to those working in these fields of human existence and are usually a pale shade of what is actually happening in the real world and even after 30 years in the "Psychiatrists chair" I am still frequently astounded at the unique and unusual real life stories that I am told which are beyond the usual meaning of eccentricity.

WHAT WILL BE WILL BE... OR WILL IT?
Compelled to Choose

The concept of free will has been an enigma for philosophers and other thinkers for many centuries. Are we programmed so that every time we are faced with a decision the response is predictable and predetermined or do we really have a genuine option of choice? When faced with the menu in my favourite restaurant, should I select the steak au poivre or would I prefer a change and try the cold chicken salad? At that micro-second in time do I really have the luxury of independent choice, unfettered by previous experience and conditioning or am I programmed by an inner inescapable determined mechanistic algorithm of which I am totally unaware like the emotionless computer that sits silently before me as I write.

Dear reader, if you find this a troublesome matter, then consider the plight of Trevor whose dilemma of choice is not only more complex but also very disabling.

It was early summer. Trevor awoke at 7.00 a.m. and could see blue sky and sunshine through a small gap in his curtains. He had slept fitfully but fairly soundly since midnight, and although feeling rested, he was aware of a sensation of inner urgency and unease pressing him to get out of his bed. After a few seconds of contemplation, he rubbed his eyes, shuffled across to the dressing table and took out two bottles of medication labelled Diazepam and Lorazepam. Both containers were closed with childproof screw-caps which he expertly pushed down and twisted off. After extracting a couple of pills from each bottle, he replaced the lids and swallowed the medication in one gulp with the aid of a glass of water carefully measured from the tap in the small adjacent sink. Next, he surveyed the selection of toiletries, brush, comb, sun-oil, toothpaste and other sundry items on the dresser. With a slight tremor, he moved the hairbrush a couple of millimetres as in his estimation, it was slightly out of line with the adjacent red comb. Irritatingly (or so it seemed to Trevor), the straight edge of the brush handle now seemed not quite parallel with the edge of the dresser.

As he was about to move again, he experienced the familiar inner tension telling himself how stupid and unnecessary it was to have every object on his dressing table lined up in such a precise and rigid pattern. He dragged himself away and sat on the edge of his bed, resisting and desperately trying not to give in to the overwhelming urge to re-arrange yet again all the toiletry objects in the special, magical order that only he knew about.

The anxiety was overwhelming, but he knew that if he waited a few minutes, the tablets would modify the terrible inner compulsion and he could then go to the kitchen and have breakfast. Not only was Trevor unable to function during the day without his tranquillizers, they were also vital for his escape from life into the sanctuary of sleep during the all too brief hours of darkness. A couple of minutes later, he heard his mother setting the breakfast table, and he rose to his feet and dressed. Unfortunately, even dressing was a major performance. Despite being a warm morning, he only required jeans and a short-sleeved shirt but the garments had to be put on in a special way. Not only did the right leg have go into the underpants and trousers first followed by the right arm in the shirtsleeve, Trevor was also compelled by his self-imposed rules to count up to 10 for manoeuvre each for each garment involved. If any of the clothes took a count too short or too many, they had to be taken off and the whole process recommenced.

This morning all went well and only the shirt ritual required to be repeated a second time. Finally, before going to the kitchen, he shook the lightweight chequered quilt and replaced it neatly on his bed. The onlooker would see it as being neat and squarely placed, awaiting evening and the next night's sleep. Such acceptance was denied to Trevor as there was a slight crease where the duvet met the underlying pillow, and Trevor gently smoothed it out with the palm of his hand. Whilst this removed the offending line, it created a telltale elevation of the underlying pillow which could only be removed by pulling the hidden pillow at each end (Trevor was an expert at this).

Unfortunately, this manoeuvre if executed too roughly (as on this occasion) caused a sideways movement of the quilt which then had to be re-aligned once again. Trevor hated this bed covering. Sometimes the compulsive ritual (which he recognized as totally silly) would take him half-hour to complete, and he once confessed to a nurse that on one occasion, he had wasted more than an hour trying to get it perfectly symmetrical.

Eventually, Trevor tore himself away from the bed and despite an overwhelming urge to go back and re-check it, he opened the bedroom door by turning the handle which he held with the aid of a Kleenex tissue (for fear of contamination), taken from a conveniently situated box on a small table. After opening the door, he counted backwards from 5, and on the count of zero, stepped smartly out onto the tiled floor of the corridor. His anxiety had now modified and there was only the bathroom rituals to overcome before joining his mum in the kitchen.

The bathroom was always a problem. Urinating was fairly straightforward but the position of his feet was critical. No matter how urgent was his urge, he would not allow himself to commence until he could see (by looking down) that neither of his feet crossed the lines between the tiles. Fortunately, the pale pink squares were larger than his feet, but unless one was vigilant, it was all too easy to misjudge the position and see the big or small toe just over the offending line. Sitting on the toilet could be very anxiety-provoking, as it was necessary to wipe the seat first to ensure it was absolutely clean and dry. This, Trevor did with a cloth which sat on the U-bend beneath the small sink.

On completing this ritual, the cloth itself had to be washed properly in the sink and then his hands had to be washed separately, carefully using the small nail-brush to ensure that no germs could possibly be left under his rather badly bitten nails.

Today was a reasonably average morning. It had only taken 30 minutes from waking to arriving at the breakfast table. He had negotiated all the rituals reasonably satisfactorily, and was feeling only moderately anxious as he sat down at the table. His mother, familiar with his rituals and obsessions, had placed everything on the table in the order and alignment that Trevor usually insisted upon: the milk jug (handle to the right) was just in front and to the left of the sugar bowl, and the jam jar stood alone about 2 cms in front of the dessert spoon handle. His mother knew from experience that if she wanted to keep him in good humour, it was vital to comply with his wishes no matter how bizarre they might appear. If she failed or attempted to challenge or thwart any of his obsessional demands, he would become cross, surly, bad-tempered and at times even threatening her with physical violence. A few weeks previously, she was so frightened that she asked him to leave the house and took out a legal restraining order.

She knew that shortly after breakfast, he would return to the backroom where he might spend up to an hour. She was unaware of the complex washing and showering rituals that Trevor followed. These involved a special order of washing, commencing with the hair for an exact period of time before switching to various other parts of the body for a further fixed routine. She had no idea that soap, towel, mat and garments all had to be hung and placed in exact locations around the room, nor was she aware that he required two towels: one for the upper and the other for the lower part of his body. Furthermore, the top and bottom of each towel was used for drying particular parts of the body and both back and front were also specific to certain areas. In fact, his mum was usually relieved when he disappeared into the bathroom because she knew that when he finally emerged, tense yet shining and clean, it was only a short time before he would commence vacuuming and cleaning.

Vacuuming and cleaning were not the perfunctory rapid going-over domestic rituals that an average 27 year old would do to please his mother. Trevor would plug in the Hoover and meticulously vacuum every inch of the carpet and tiled floor. Each room was subjected to careful, geometrically-planned patterning so that not even a tiny patch under the heavy leather sofa (which had to be moved) would miss the beating, sweeping and cleaning of the droning electrical appliance. The whole process could take over an hour. Occasionally, after completing the whole house, he would return to an earlier room for a "touch-up" because he might have missed "an odd corner or two".

On special days (she never quite knew which they were), Trevor would give a repeat house hoovering in the late afternoon as well as the morning session. A few weeks earlier, there was a crisis. About 1.30 in the afternoon, Trevor was half-way through the hoovering when there was a flash of light which came from inside the body of the machine followed by a strong smell of burning rubber. Fiddling with the wires and wriggling the plug was in vain. The machine was broken due to a burnt-out motor. Rather than solving Trevor's vacuuming compulsion, this mechanical failure created a sense of panic and overwhelming urgency. Logically, he was aware that there was no real threat from the dust mites and bacteria lurking in the dark recesses of the carpet pile, but simultaneously he was aware of a persistent and overwhelming doubt that there might just be one or two virulent germs waiting for the opportunity to invade.

This illogical doubt finally overwhelmed his common sense and rational resistance, and when the man at the electrical shop informed him that repairs would take at least two days, he knew he could not last, so the next day he hired another cleaner. Being unable to find a small domestic type, and to his mother's horror, he returned home with a large commercial model designed especially for cleaning large offices, workshops and warehouses. This was a splendid machine with a powerful engine with a satisfying force of suction that could rapidly and greedily swallow objects the size of marbles and broken biros. The sense of gratification it evoked in Trevor was far superior to the old Hoover that his mum had received as a wedding present nearly 30 years ago.

His mother was overwhelmed by the frightening noise of this cleansing Leviathan, and after 10 minutes, lost her self-control completely and wrenched the plug from the electrical power socket. She screamed and informed Trevor that she could no longer tolerate his behaviours, rituals and compulsions. She gave him 24 hours to leave the house and find somewhere else to live. This was the third time in 18 months that such a crisis had occurred, and as on a previous occasion, she obtained a protection order preventing his return to the house. After a few weeks, Trevor convinced her that he was better and taking medication, and if she allowed him to return home, he would behave normally and commence to look for work.

Within days, he had returned to a full programme of bizarre rituals, compulsions and intrusive behaviours. A young nurse from the Community Mental Health Team visited her at home and counselled her about Trevor's condition, and suggested some coping strategies. This had helped a little, but the memory of the monster vacuum cleaner was just too much, and before long, Trevor and his mother were accusing each other of mutually inconsiderate behaviours and a general lack of personal tolerance. When glass objects commenced being used as missiles and his mother ran out into the street

14

screaming and shouting, the neighbours (who were already partly aware of the problem) phoned the police who in turn called for the Psychiatric Emergency Team who promptly arranged for Trevor to be involuntarily admitted to the local Psychiatric Unit.

Obsessive compulsive disorder (O.C.D) is an illness which in a mild form affects at least one in a hundred people. It is not to be confused with those normal people whom we all recognize and know amongst our friends and relatives as being perfectionistic, obsessional and at times rather rigid. Mild obsessive compulsive disorder is probably very common, and both the afflicted and their families have learned to accept and live with some of the odd behaviours and rituals. Sufferers may experience a variety of symptoms. The central fault is difficult to identify as several systems are involved. Unwanted thoughts, ideas, illogical urges or memories intrude into the person's consciousness. These obsessional ruminations, as they are sometimes called, are recognized as being both uninvited and out of context, being resisted by the sufferer in a similar manner to that which we all adopt when trying not to avoid treading on cracks in the pavement or from humming or whistling a persistent tune in our minds. Unfortunately, this conscious act of resisting reinforces the alien thoughts, resulting in their persistence, creating more anxiety and frustration. The sufferer then develops special methods which are believed will help in eliminating the obsessions. These strategies may involve touching or not touching certain objects, performing unusual movements with the arms or body, or by counting or arranging objects in a particular order. These behaviours which seem meaningless and bizarre to the outsider, have almost magical significance to the executor, and are referred to as rituals. Some of course are understandable such as the person who spends half-hour checking that the electrical switches and gas taps are switched off. Others have doubts that their hands have been correctly washed after touching what might be a dirty door handle.

Irrational fears are also common and include a constant checking and re-checking of appliances "just in case they have forgotten one".

Sometimes, these rituals become multiple and complex and have to be followed through an elaborate sequence. The urge to comply with and perform these behaviours is overwhelming and it is only when these compulsions are completed that there is a temporary sense of relief before the urge gradually returns.

Perhaps the cruellest aspect of obsessive compulsive disorder is that the person is aware of the illogical, intrusive and irrational nature of the obsessions, urges, rituals and doubts, and despite enormous mental effort, finally surrenders to their overwhelming power. The individual's autonomy and personal freedom to choose how to behave is severely afflicted. In this sense, it is truly a disorder of the will.

Trevor always knew his behaviours were silly. He knew they were irrational, but the inner compulsion which constantly drove him to execute them never ceased. The pills he took sometimes modified the anxiety and helped him escape into sleep. Alcohol in the form of beer also took away the intensity enabling him to interact socially with old friends. During three lengthy stays in hospital, psychologists had taught him some strategies for combatting his symptoms. Sadly, all these were only temporary escapes, and he remained permanently tortured. On two occasions, he became so desperate in his quest to escape that he took large overdoses of medications and was rushed to the Emergency Department for resuscitation and admission to Intensive Care.

The cause of obsessive compulsive disorder is unclear. A few years ago, it was regarded as a neurotic illness in the same category as depression and anxiety, but recent advances in diagnostic technologies strongly suggest that it is a brain disorder in which certain basic deep structures and nervous pathways in the brain are somehow out of balance. Certain medications provide considerable relief to some sufferers, others gain much relief from carefully planned behaviour therapy programmes. Unfortunately, there are still only a few centres which offer these treatments, and there is little relief for many of these unfortunate people who suffer silently, and yet superficially may seem to be quite normal.

PHYLLIS AND THE AXE MAN

The doctors' residences consisted of eight grey semi-detached hospital houses in a line. The back doors and gardens looked southwards across the pleasant patchwork of green fields and farmland. On a fine day, in the far distance, glimpses of the English Channel could be seen between two valleys glinting in the sunshine. Northwards, the neatly painted front doors and aluminium windows faced the slopes of Dartmoor whose colours varied through a seasonal spectrum of greys, greens, purples, browns and the dazzling whites of fresh winter snow.

In front of the row of manicured bordered lawns was a narrow private lane serving the multiple purposes of children's play area, car parking, and a conversation ground for the wives and families of the doctors who worked in the hospital further up the hill. The lane was also a convenient pitch for mobile tradesmen, at least one of whom would visit each day. In fact after one had lived in the Close (as it was suitably named) for a while, the original pagan names were synonymous with fish day, greengrocer day, library day or butcher day according to who was responsible for supplying the vital supplies on that particular morning.

In addition to delivering our daily supplies, the mobile shops also served as a focus for social interaction especially for the women and children of the Close in similar fashion to the village wells of medieval times. As in all social systems, there inevitably evolves a hierarchy in which certain individuals attempt by some means or other to acquire a superior or an elitist position. The rationalization for this may be obvious and incontestable such as wealth, a Mercedes Benz parked outside or perhaps some aspect of rank or professional status. In the absence of such obvious yet dubious advantages, the individual seeking superiority will inevitably find some symbolic object or phenomenon on which to score a few points on the personal superiority scale.

At the top of the Close, lived Phyllis and Joe who were a few years older than other residents. They had also lived in the Close longer, but the principal difference was that unlike everyone else, they were childless. Consequently, Phyllis was unable to take part in much of the discussion involving children, playgroups and school dancing classes etc..., discussions which occurred as the women chose and selected the fish or meat for the evening meal.

Phyllis had discovered a significant difference in their residence which the rest of us did not share. Each hospital house was furnished identically, including a small solid fuel heater in the kitchen, ensuring a cozy warm atmosphere even in the depths of the cold Dartmoor winters. Unfortunately, there was no heating in the other rooms, thus condemning them as chilly, inhospitable and uninhabitable unless additional expensive heating appliances were installed. Not so in Phyllis's house! Some time before our arrivals in the Close, Joe had persuaded the hospital's management committee that for "medical reasons", a radiator should be plumbed into the back of the kitchen stove and through the wall to the adjacent sitting-room. We never discovered the nature or severity of the medical disability for it never appeared very obvious to the onlooker. Nevertheless, this extra radiator, this unquestioned symbol of luxury became an object of superiority and accomplishment and an irritating source of envy and covetousness for the other women whose children had to co-exist in the kitchen whilst Joe and Phyllis could sit tranquilly in the relative warmth of the lounge reading and relaxing with a degree of comfort.

Approximately 15 miles to the north of the Close and its line of cozy cottages, was the small town of Princeton and the adjacent Dartmoor Jail where some of the country's more difficult and dangerous criminals were detained for lengthy periods at her Majesty's pleasure.

One day, we were alarmed to learn that a certain Frank Mitchell had escaped from an outside working party and was on the run. The local radio advised us to keep our doors, windows and garages locked at all times as Mitchell was said to be dangerous and had a long history of violence. He had a reputation for using an axe with great dexterity in many of his criminal activities. The whole community was thus in a state of fear on learning that the "Axe Man" (as he was usually referred to) was now at large. In addition to staying home during hours of darkness, most of us kept some weapon for reassurance such as a poker or a frying-pan under the bed just in case it was our residence that he chose for his own evil purposes. On reflection, these safeguards would have been almost useless, but they did provide a reassuring placebo sensation of safety.

Thus, a whole week-end was spent under a cloud of apprehension and hypervigilance which increased the longer he remained at large, as we imagined that his feelings of desperation would be augmented directly in proportion to his time on the run. A visit to the coal shed, dustbin or even the outside toilet, normally unemotional excursions, required a minor degree of courage and caution.

At approximately 10.30 on Monday morning, the travelling greengrocer's truck growled up the steep hill in low gear, filling the air with diesel fumes, and turned into the Close. The proprietor drew back the tarpaulin shutters so that the ladies of the Close could browse and make their purchases. As they gathered, there was an extra element of excitement to their discussion not usually evident on a Monday morning, and of course Frank Mitchell was the central topic.

Unfortunately, Phyllis and Joe had been on a week's holiday and were consequently unaware of the heightened tension and excitement which had built up in the community. After an exchange of information about the relative usefulness of a coal axe kept by the bedside compared to placing the wardrobe behind the bedroom door, it became obvious that Phyllis was oblivious to the local drama. Sensing her reluctance to acknowledge ignorance of recent local events, my wife mischievously asked her directly: "Have you seen the Axe Man yet?" Delighted that she had now been included in the morning's discussion group, yet still unaware of the topic, she smiled with relief but unfortunately having picked up the wrong cue, asked in a confident and understanding tone " No, I haven't seen him yet. What day does he visit?"

Footnote: *Fortunately for us (but regrettably for Mitchell), we learned later that his escape from Dartmoor had been skillfully organised by the London underworld who subsequently silenced him for ever, thus ensuring his long-term confidentiality...*

THE MYSTERY OF CHARISMA

Charisma, like love, nostalgia and consciousness is a human attribute that exists, yet we have no idea as to its essence or origins, nor can it be measured. Somehow we just recognise its presence in special individuals and we can sense it's uncanny power upon ourselves when we are under the influence of a charismatic personality.

There is a dearth of research and no scientific study on charisma as a measurable personality trait. The term originated from new testament Greek and means The Gift of Grace but modern sociologists define it as ,"an extraordinary quality possessed by certain persons endowing them with unique, persuasive qualities and interpersonal power." The concept can be divided into individual charisma arising from the personal qualities of an individual and the charisma arising out of high of office which derives from the sacred, magical or hallowed nature of the position itself. Prime Ministers, Presidents, Popes and Senior Judges come to mind. When both elements occur together charisma may become a revolutionary force which can be to either the advantage or disadvantage of the group or community over which they have influence.

HITLER: LEST WE FORGET

Very occasionally the process of human evolution produces individuals whose talents and abilities are extraordinarily different from those of the average person. These extremely unusual and creative people leave behind them music, literature and great works of art which we continue to admire and recognise as products of genius centuries after the originators have died. Unfortunately, counterbalancing the uniqueness of these men and women are other talented individuals who see themselves as being chosen, earnestly believing that it is their life's mission to radically change the society into which they have been born, and see their role in life as being to purify, improve or save the lot of the people.

Driven by insatiable zeal and an infectious charisma these rare individuals sweep aside the accepted conventions of privacy and law in the name of revolution and a change for a better society. Historians and sociologists tell us that these people flourish at certain critical times such as when a population is dissatisfied, disgruntled, affluently bored or in a state of spiritual poverty. In such situations social upheaval, irrational behaviour and political turmoil are likely to occur, resulting in anarchy and the breakdown of established order. Such names as Idi Amin, Saddam Hussein, Stalin, Pol Pot and Napoleon come to mind and have all been the subject of research and enquiry. But the most destructive, democratically elected man in the last hundred years was Adolf Hitler.

ONE MAN'S MADNESS. A WORLD OF SUFFERING
I never met Hitler, yet somehow I feel I have known him all

my life. As a small boy I remember with great clarity sitting uncomfortably in a deck chair, its legs half an inch deep in muddy water in the gloomy depths of the low ceilinged cellar of our little semi-detached house in Sheffield. Above could be heard the distant drone of aeroplanes coming to drop their explosive loads on the city's steelworks. This was one of many early experiences which we as children were taught were just part of the evil associated with Hitler and his war. To us, the words Hitler and evil were synonymous and associated with revulsion, fear and disgust, even though we were too young to appreciate the sinister significance of what was really happening.

Adolf Hitler was without doubt the most influential and disruptive individual in the Western World during the twentieth century, and no other human being has been responsible for damaging or destroying so many lives or has generated so much hatred and fear, the long-term effects of which are still globally apparent. A persistent and stubborn reminder of this malignant post-war turmoil and ever-present emotional scarring is to be heard daily in the real-life stories told by thousands of depressed, damaged and traumatised people who seek psychological counselling and psychiatric assistance in clinics and hospitals around the world. These unhappy, distressed people in constant psychic pain are the relatives and descendants of concentration camp victims, firing squads, torture and disrupted families. They are the refugees still grieving for the loss of country, culture, language and the ancestral home which no longer exists. Because of the passage of time it is all too easy to forget that these people stigmatised as patients and clients carry the unhealing scars manifest as depression, anxiety, substance abuse and endless despair which are a consequence and legacy of the distorted ideas and actions of one fanatical, extraordinarily illogical mind. Whilst it is true that there were many others who shared his views, he was the charismatic figure who, by his powerful and frightening rhetoric, persuaded an entire nation to comply with his policies of genocide and extermination and his ultimate goal of world domination. Over many years of listening to hundreds of histories of these unhappy damaged patients I have become painfully aware of the persistent trans generational thread leading back to the initial precipitating and causal origin, i.e. the mind of Hitler. Consequently this has provoked me to reflect on what so many others have already pondered. What sort of person was he? Why did he think and behave in this grossly irrational and destructive manner, and could some or all of his ideas and behaviour be manifestations of what today would be classified as mental illness or personality disorder? It is fascinating to speculate whether or not, if he was mentally ill, was the illness of such a nature and degree that he would be considered a danger to himself or others and thus should be certified under current mental health legislation for assessment and treatment in an approved institution. If this had been done at the time, how different the history of the world would have been!

The Hitler conundrum is a twofold mystery and any tentative explanation requires an understanding both of why Hitler thought and behaved in the way he did and secondly why so many people not only supported his ideas but actually participated willingly in his destructive and genocidal activities.

HITLER THE MAN
Following Hitler's suicide an international team of five psychiatrists and psychologists were commissioned to investigate and report their findings in an attempt to explain the complexities of his mental functioning. Since then there have been hundreds or publications and papers and books by famous students of human behaviour but it is probably true that there is no unanimous, precise conclusion or diagnostic agreement.

BACKGROUND

Although of German parentage he was born in a small town in Austria where his father was a civil servant. Childhood friends report that Hitler was always a serious boy and 'at odds with the world'. Once, on his way home from a Wagnerian opera, he confided to a friend that one day he was going to save his country. So there is evidence of his zealous patriotism from an early age.

It is no secret that Hitler hated his father, who was reported to be a drunkard, a tyrant and a wifebeater. Hitler believed his father to have been the illegitimate child of his grandfather and a Jewish domestic servant, a fact that some analysts have used to explain his exaggerated prejudice and loathing of Jewish people. Hitler was very attached to and protective of his mother (who was 23 years younger than his father) and when she died he became very depressed and exhibited what would nowadays be described as pathological mourning. Predictably, some psychoanalysts have not unreasonably theorised that much of his subsequent behaviour was an unconscious symbolic wish to destroy his internalised father and to protect and save his mother. The theory has some support from the observation that most of his speeches made striking use of parental and family imagery. Others have commented that all his three brothers died in infancy, reinforcing his belief in his personal invincibility and omnipotence.

SOME ABNORMAL SYMPTOMS

During his life Hitler demonstrated features highly suggestive of a grossly abnormal personality and of mental illness. In the First World War he fought in the trenches and later described this horrendous experience as 'the best time in my life'. In 1918 he was severely gassed, a fact that some neurologists have hypothesised could have irreversibly damaged the sensitive frontal parts of his brain.

Hitler frequently expressed extreme guilt over ideas of

incest and would accuse others of this perversion as a way of self-appeasement. This obsession was probably augmented by his torrid relationship with his niece who, coincidentally, was 23 years his junior. He once claimed that she was the only true love in his life and after she committed suicide he became riven with guilt, self-punitive ideas, and cut off one of his testicles. He was preoccupied with dirt, germs and contamination, washing his hair at least once a day, changing his underwear twice daily. He scrubbed his hands until they were sore. He was over-concerned about bodily odours and became a vegetarian because he believed eating meat caused unpleasant flatulence which he attempted to control by taking large quantities of Dr Gostershain's 'anti-gas pills'. The concept of inner purity was a constant preoccupation. Most of his adult life he was known to suffer from depression, uncontrollable mood swings, despair, self-loathing, suicidal ideas, anxiety and chronic insomnia. He intensely disliked tying his tie, which was usually done for him by a valet, a task which had to be completed in less than ten seconds whilst Hitler held his breath. If the process took longer he would become very anxious and irritable. He had an unpredictable explosive temper, a fiery personality, marked theatrical traits and at times was capable of long, tireless periods of hard creative work. Not surprisingly he had no close personal friends.

Perhaps the most socially destructive symptoms that Hitler experienced were those delusional ideas involving his own grandiosity, omnipotence and a conviction that he was 'chosen' to be the saviour of his country. There are hundreds of recorded utterances attesting to this. In Mein Kampf, for example, he wrote 'Hence today I believe that I am acting in accordance with the will of the almighty creator. By defending myself against the Jew I am fighting for the work of the Lord.' On another occasion he likened himself to Jesus Christ, saying that 'Who Thou art Thou art to me and all I am I am to Thee'. This unquestioned and insightless messianic belief in his own importance was clearly of a delusional nature but became of central importance when he was able to convince others of the validity of these ideas by his great skills as a persuasive orator. It is known that he learned these techniques from a trained oratory teacher and would then practise his speeches out loud for hours beforehand. There is no doubting his messianic charisma, which influenced the masses into an almost trance-like state by commencing slowly and gradually, increasing the tempo of his delivery and becoming faster and louder and then adding his well-practised bodily gestures and hypnotic arm raising movements.

DRUGS

Because of his obsession with cleanliness and inner purity Hitler denied himself alcohol or tobacco. But later in life, as he began to lose self-control, he commenced using sedatives and sleeping drugs of the barbiturate class. These are addictive drugs and before long he became dependent upon them and as often occurs soon resorted to amphetamine pills ('speed') to give himself more energy and to counter the sedative effects of the barbiturates. Predictably, the effect of oral medications became insufficient so his physician commenced him on the more potent intravenous forms and towards the end of his life required four or five intravenous injections daily. A common complication of amphetamine use is that it often causes a paranoid disorder and the addict acquires delusional ideas of persecution, grandiosity and invincibility. Consequently, Hitler's pre-existing delusional beliefs would have been augmented and perpetuated by amphetamine usage requiring energetic medical treatment to prevent further escalation of symptoms.

CHARISMA

The broad outlines of Hitler's medical and psychiatric history are not in doubt but the psychological and social mechanisms whereby he was able to indoctrinate and intimidate millions of intelligent and ordinary people to such a degree that their minds were manipulated and controlled are still ill understood. Somehow Hitler had the frightening ability to induce feelings of childlike inspiration, obedience and irrational loyalty, and any opposition or attempt to refute his ideas would provoke a complex sense of shame and fear.

Charisma is a well recognised gift of great orators, political leaders, spiritual evangelists and modem pop stars. Winston Churchill, Gandhi, Billy Graham and Elvis Presley are examples of some of these people possessing this distinctive and potent trait.

Charisma seems to be a form of group hypnosis in which the critical faculties become lost in the crowd. One is reminded of the states in which people can temporarily be persuaded to enter into a trance and behave in a bizarre manner quite out of keeping with their usual personality style. There is also an unusual yet well known psychiatric disorder called *folie a deux* in which a mental illness develops in a person who is in a close relationship with someone else, already suffering from mental disorder. When the second 'infected' person leaves the relationship for some reason, they return to normal functioning, leaving the other 'genuinely ill' person unchanged. There are many examples of large groups of people being persuaded to adopt ideas and behaviours quite out of keeping with their previous personalities. Perhaps the most horrific example in recent times was when the Reverend Jim Jones persuaded 913 people to commit mass murder/suicide in Guyana in 1978 after persuading them to take cyanide as they were all 'destined to be saved for eternal life'. No amount of research or hypothesising has given a satisfactory solution as to why there appeared to be no real opposition to his lethal demands.

In our era of scientific reasoning it is heretical to admit that we do not understand or cannot explain, and there is a constant intellectual danger of treating what is really vague as if it were precise. Our understanding of the nature of personal charisma is an example of this illusion of precision. This vagueness and imprecision about personal charisma extends to our lack of understanding of the reasons why at certain times large groups of people such as crowds, communities, and even a whole country can somehow come under the spell of the powerful charismatic individual.

Many psychologists, sociologists and political theorists have pondered and written on this elusive topic but it is probably true to say that no consistent explanation yet exists. There is general agreement that under certain conditions an individual can change and come to understand, think, feel and act in a way different from the manner in which he/she would behave as an individual, but just why this should occur defies logical explanation. A group can somehow transform all its members into possessing a sort of collective mind or consciousness, causing each to act in a manner quite different from that in which they would behave in a state of isolation. This group mind as it is frequently called is facilitated by several factors each of which play a role influencing the individual's autonomy. Membership of a group led by an inspirational leader induces a sense of shared invincible power in the individual that is not possible in isolation, where one is open to criticism and intellectual challenge. The group provides anonymity (safety in numbers), which effectively diminishes the sense of personal accountability and responsibility.

CONTAGION AND SUGGESTIBILITY
Contagion by ideas and behaviour from other members of a group and the leader are powerful forces causing surrender of personal to the collective interests. These factors evoke a heightened sense of suggestibility, resulting in lowering the individual's critical faculty. Most writers on the 'Group Mind' agree that the larger the group the greater becomes the suggestibility and vulnerability of its members to the beliefs and ideas of a charismatic leader. Hitler made great use of this size factor, and many of his speeches were amplified to crowds

in excess of a hundred thousand people, already in a state of high suggestibility due to a prologue of singing and stirring military music.

Whilst we recognize that contagion and suggestibility are central in facilitating the charismatic leader's message, we do not understand how or why. Shifting the explanation to the riddle of hypnosis is also unsatisfactory as there is still no solution to the hypnotic phenomenon itself.

Long before Hitler was born the French sociologist Le Bon wrote:

'By the fact he forms part of an organised group a man descends several rungs on the ladder of civilisation. Isolated, he may be a cultured individual. In a crowd he is a barbarian descending to the spontaneity, the violence, the ferocity and the enthusiasm of primitive beings.'

This analysis certainly describes a large element of the Hitler charisma phenomenon.

There are other psychoanalytical and sociological theories attempting to explain the charismatic phenomenon. One popular hypothesis suggests that although we demand personal freedom and autonomy at a conscious level, unconsciously we cannot cope with freedom, hence the tendency to escape by submission to a charismatic leader and totalitarian rule.

These are complex psycho-social issues involving the reciprocal relationship between individuals and the communities in which they live, hence raising complex questions which so far have been the subject of much speculation but no serious or conclusive research.

In conclusion, I believe that until social scientists and psychologists have a clearer understanding of the nature and multiple aspects of charisma, especially its more destructive properties, it is of increasing importance that at annual ceremonies of remembrance for those who died in two world wars we should also remember the name of Hitler, for this symbolises the primitive, instinctual, destructive forces which somehow lie festering in the dark, inaccessible parts of the human psyche that Freud referred to as the Id which like seeds in the desert lie dormant until a favourable environmental change permits them to spring into life once again.

As those of us who lived through the dark years of the last world war decrease in number, the risk of forgetting the name of Hitler and all its vile associations increases correspondingly. We will never know when or where the next Hitler will appear, but if we forget him there is no reason why another charismatic psychotic individual will not once again lead us back into the miseries and destructive gloom which enveloped the whole world in the middle of the last century.

CHRISTMAS: BAHAMAS 1970
"A time to remember those less fortunate than ourselves"

Thankfully Christmas comes but once a year, and the complex culture bound packages of behaviours, attitudes and emotions commence slowly and imperceptibly towards the end of October, and then accelerate to a disinhibited climax of consumerism and television spectaculars late on Christmas Day. The Bahamian sequence of events is no exception and has its own particular cultural flavour.

The British Commonwealth system has left an indelible stamp of its earlier presence. Railways, legal systems, water supply, sewerage, and public health systems still function in approximately the same manner as they did when the Union Jacks were pulled down and the British moved out. There are many less obvious vestiges of this era, and many complex rituals and social behaviours, introduced by the previous colony, are firmly and ambivalently woven into the annual calendar of events. The Yuletide ritual is one of these persistent and powerful remnants and an example is to be experienced a few days before Christmas at Sandilands Hospital.

Sandilands Psychiatric Hospital was built in the early 50s about 5 miles to the east of Nassau town. A sprawling, single-storeyed concrete building with bars in the glassless windows, Sandilands was taken off the "architecture peg" of the overseas development office in London. It is a mirror image building with male and female wards separated by the administration, treatment and workshop blocks. The bare ward areas face into two large unpaved courtyards in the centre of which grows a majestic large king palm tree. Following tropical rainstorms, these courtyards became spattered with puddles of brown fetid water in which would float cigarette butts, old metal cans and the occasional rejected crust of stale bread. As the warm rain poured

down, mournful eyes of the depressed, the psychotic and the intellectually handicapped would gaze out through the bars of their locked enclosure, euphemistically referred to as "wards". In the heat of summer, the ground would become dry, hard and dusty, and when the wind swirled round the courtyard, rubbish would circulate, in an invisible whirlpool of wind.

Ward staff consisted of a few trained dutiful nurses assisted by a larger body of white coated attendants who had been given some minimal instruction into the basics of caring for the psychiatrically ill. Apart from the more recently built alcohol treatment unit, the four major treatment wards were locked at all times. This was despite many attempts to convince staff that, with the correct use of modern medication, patient selection and occupational therapy programmes, patient management would actually have been easier and more therapeutic. It is a fascinating thought that the large locks securing the heavy doors at Sandilands Hospital were identical to those on hundreds of other similar doors on the closed wards at colonial style hospitals around the entire world and could be opened by one large heavy key, marked "Chubb" of Wolverhampton, which if carried in the pocket for too long would result in an obvious lump at the front of the trousers, which with time wore away the fabric, resulting in an embarrassing and irregular hole.

Alternatively, one could carry the key on a ring attached to the trouser belt, but this gave the impression of being a jailer rather than a health care worker. Despite these physical restraints imposed by the adoption of obsolete architectural plans from a previous custodial era, the hospital manager to serve a useful function, and there was a happy, positive and energetic approach amongst staff to the treatment and rehabilitation of the severely ill and socially disadvantaged section of the Bahamian community. An outpatient clinic had been opened at the downtown Princess Margaret Hospital, an occupational therapy service had commenced and an active Bahamas Mental Health Association organised public awareness meetings and an annual mental health week. An energetic group of people, known as "the Friends of Sandilands", had contributed towards many facilities including a swimming pool. Young, recently qualified people (commonly known as expatriates) bored by the thought of forty years' work in Britain and seeking adventurous challenges, threw themselves into service with zest and energy as they worked on 3-year overseas contracts. What they lacked in experience was more than compensated for by this "elan vital" and enthusiasm.

The approach to Sandilands Hospital was unimpressive and concealed some of the less attractive features behind the hospital walls. A tarmac road lined with majestic tall palms led around the perimeter of an uneven crab-grass oval which was used on special occasions such as open days and sports days. However, it was at Christmas time that for several hours, the Sandilands oval became the centre of activity. The Friends of Sandilands erected trestle tables and arranged a sale of work from the occupational therapy department. Local Bahamian delicacies, cooking and preserves could also be bought and used for last minute presents. The less disturbed patients were "allowed out" and encouraged to participate in activities such as the tug-of-war, bursting balloons or skittles. A few of the younger ones would be persuaded to play the "slippery pole" in which contestants were sat astride a polished horizontal pole facing each other armed with pillows, the aim of the contest being the first to fell one's opponent onto the straw mattress below. This of course was to the merriment of surrounding spectators and seemed to me to be a contest enjoyed more by onlookers than participants.

Adding to the excitement, was the presence of the Royal Bahamas Police Force band, being a body of about thirty men, resplendent in tropical white uniforms and military hats, who had been expertly trained and tutored by the Welsh Director of Music. The band would march backwards and forwards, in formation, criss-crossing the oval, playing such non-Bahamian tunes as "Sussex by the Sea", "Tipperary" and "Little Brown Jug", before launching into a medley of well known Christmas carols. As they proudly traversed the centre of the oval, they would rise and fall and occasionally stumble due to the uneven ground and the presence of small pot-holes concealed beneath the coarse crab-grass. Local dignitaries, health department officials, relatives and staff would all mingle, sharing in the fun and those unique sensations of goodwill which are unique to the few remaining days of Advent.

These activities and light-hearted excesses were only a prelude to the major event. They were a social overture to the principal happening, which we were all waiting with differing emotions. The peak of the day was the visit of the Governor and the official party, and the traditional speech by the Governor's wife to the assembled company. Portable telephones were not available in the early 70s so no one knew exactly when the official party would arrive, which enhanced the excitement and anticipation. The ambiance of expectancy was augmented a few minutes before by the appearance of the advance party who arrived in an open Land Rover. A small Union Jack flapped on a short mast on the front mud-guard and the senior police sergeant would be standing in the front seat wearing a polished brown leather belt and carrying a shiny wooden baton with brass end tips.

Finally the white Austin Princess arrived and glided smoothly round the perimeter before coming to a halt outside the main entrance. The police sergeant would step smartly forwards, open the rear door, salute, and permit the Governor and his wife to alight and cross to the small wooden platform under the lea of a large silk cotton tree. People clapped and cheered enthusiastically as the band launched into "God Save the Queen".

The Governor was a tall, slim man who wore an immaculately pressed white suit with a red handkerchief in his top pocket. On his head, he sported an expensive straw hat bent jauntily over the front brim. As at most public ceremonies, he was accompanied by his wife who was an ever-smiling buxom, middle-aged, jolly lady wearing a light blue English summer dress and white shoes. Her bright red lipstick and matching earrings seemed apparent, but this was outshone by her splendid hat. This had a wide brim concealed by a red band above which was an assortment of tropical fruit which from a distance could not be distinguished as real or artificial. After smiling, chatting and shaking lots of eager hands with the officials and staff, the Governor moved to the large microphone to address us all.

In loud, confident, clear English sonorous tones, clearly identifying his ex English public school origins and, as he spoke, he flapped his arms from side to side as the milkman does on a cold morning in order to warm his hands. At this point, many of us would begin to cringe in anticipation. "It is on such occasions as this that we should remember those who are much less fortunate than ourselves; those who are unable to enjoy the pleasures and the message of Christmas ..." As I listened, I wondered if he would be quite so enthusiastic and optimistic if he could actually witness the daily miseries within the confines of the wards of the hospital, hidden by the walls and the pretty ornamental hibiscus hedges that lay between us on the green sunny oval and the bare, over-crowded, windowless, mosquito-ridden wards beyond. Did he realise that there are still many patients who are too disturbed to attend the Yuletide festivities going on outside? It was at this point in his oration that the unexpected happened. As his lordship flapped his arms and began to draw parallels between good medical care and the message of Christmas, a thin, penetrating, wailing cry was heard above and beyond us all. Those of us facing the hospital could see the origins of the disturbance instantly. Those whose backs were towards the building only had to turn their heads.

A slight female figure clad only in a flimsy, flapping hospital night dress was slowly climbing up the red tile roof ridge above the female ward. It was Elsie Rolle. Elsie was well known, as her irreversibly alcohol-damaged brain made it virtually impossible to control and treat the additional longstanding manic depressive illness from which she also suffered. Unfortunately, with all attention now being focused on the Yuletide oval activities, she had slipped out of the understaffed ward, scaled a rickety drainpipe and climbed onto the roof above.

Perilously, she swayed, climbing higher and nearer to the apex of the roof, and then in a gesture of triumph and grandiosity, she waved from her elevated position to the assembled company below. All eyes which had seconds earlier been focused on his lordship had now switched to Elsie who commanded the full attention of the whole assembly. Female attendants rushed into the interior of the hospital to find a ladder, whilst the Governor skillfully brought his message of goodwill to a close by wishing all patients and staff a Merry Christmas and a Happy New Year. Dennis, the ever vigilant Welsh band leader, raised his baton and the band commenced to play "For He Is a Jolly Good Fellow". Simultaneously, a sudden discourteous gust of chilly Yuletide wind blew Elsie's nightgown up and over her head, compromising further her precarious position. Later, as we went on our way home, perhaps detouring in order to complete the last bits of Christmas shopping, many of us pondered just who exactly his lordship was referring to in his Yuletide message. Who could these people be who were "worse off" than the severely disabled patients in Sandilands Hospital? Just what afflictions or social injustices must they have endured to be categorized thus? Every Christmas, I reflect on this event and wonder whether or not the Governor ever again had the temerity to allude to that undefined group of people whom he had in mind and described as being "less fortunate than ourselves."

Footnote: Since these past colonial happenings, Sandilands Hospital has been upgraded and is now the hub of a modern community psychiatric service staffed by a well-trained multidisciplinary team of dedicated mental health workers.

HIS PERSONAL BEST
A Cautionary Tale

The true purpose and meaning of life remains a mystery to most honest and logically thinking people. Religion, philosophy, science and poetry all express their views but in the end, as Marcus Aurelius both as emperor and philosopher concluded, *"there are no facts, only opinions."* This view has been repeated many times and in different forms, a contemporary one being Carl Popper's underpinning of modern scientific method, that as we will never know the truth, the task is to create testable hypotheses in an attempt to refute them, thus creating another which hopefully will be a little nearer to the true nature of things, whatever that is.

This rather pessimistic view of the nature of existence has been the favourite topic of philosophers, psychologists and psychiatrists since the early part of the 20th century and before. The French writers have been particularly involved. One of the novel conclusions of this group of thinkers and writers is that if we cannot establish the purpose of life (and some experts believe there may not be one at all), then in order to be happy, we must invent our own meaningful goals as if they were real. Whilst this may seem by many to be a sort of sleight of hand or psychological chicanery, there are many observations strongly confirming that this is precisely how a large proportion of the human race console themselves most of the time.

Like-minded people sharing common interests, activities, beliefs and opinions, join together to share their ideas and to construct systems and networks to propagate further their field of interest and inquiry. Before long, rules for joining, belonging, membership, inclusion and exclusion criteria are established, and the inevitable and all too familiar hierarchies of seniority, committees and awards for meritorious service evolve.

The underlying dynamics of this complex behaviour are irrelevant to our present story. What is significant is that each individual who joins and participates in such a club, group, religion, fraternity or similar affiliation of like-minded people is rewarded by experiencing a sense of goal, direction and purpose. Membership is more than just sharing an interest. It gives a sense of meaning in an otherwise meaningless existence. This collective sharing eliminates the "as if' component, permitting a comforting illusion of purpose and direction.

Membership of a running club is but one of many examples of this phenomenon. During the last 50 years, running for fun has increasingly become a popular leisure activity for people of all ages. We have witnessed an explosion of jogging clubs, marathon running, fun runs, annual events attracting thousands of citizens of all ages, and the evolution of giant multinational companies producing scientifically-designed fashionable footwear, track suits and training equipment, not to mention scores of medical research papers demonstrating increased health benefits in those who engage, in regular jogging and running activities.

Those of us who commenced in the running revolution in the 1950s and 60s were often regarded as somewhat eccentric, odd and non-conformist because we preferred to trudge half-naked through mud and over moor rather than play soccer or cricket. Nowadays, the scantily-clad jogger plodding on the road or through the park is the norm, and no longer raises an eyebrow. Perhaps it was the post war mystique of the superhuman Czech, Zatopek, that kindled the public imagination or Bannister's breaking of the 4-minute mile, a barrier which for years had been regarded as beyond the capabilities of human physiology or maybe it was Chris Brasher's creation of the London Marathon for all and everyone, which triggered the collective enthusiasm to participate in what is now a global activity giving millions a sense of meaning and purpose to keep fit, to participate, to belong and to share in a common goal.

One of the interesting offshoots of last century's running revolution has been the growth of the veterans' athletic movement. Eligibility is delightfully simple: a wish to continue engaging in athletic activities or running, to be over 35 years of age and payment of a small annual subscription. Once enrolled, the runner is able to participate in a variety of local events ranging from 5-kilometre slow jogs to a longer, more arduous contest for those of a more competitive nature. Additionally, there is an international calender of veterans' events including an annual athletics' meeting somewhere in the world. Whilst the emphasis is more social and competitive, there is an established system of world record times for all events, from the 100-metre sprint to the marathon, for each 5-year age category. This cunning system enables several entrants in one event to obtain a medal or similar accolade for being first, second or third in their particular age group. Some years ago, a 71-year old Yorkshire colleague and club member entered the Veterans' 10,000 metres at the annual Birmingham meeting. A couple of weeks later, when asked how he had performed, he proudly showed his gold medal nestling snugly in a small velvet-lined box. It was only on, further inquiry that he sheepishly admitted that he had been the only entrant in the 70 75 year category!

Another curious aspect of this age-related world record system is that as the next 5-year boundary line approaches, one actually looks forward to becoming older for one moves into an age category where times are slower and more in tune with one's inevitably declining physiology and anatomical efficiency.

The preoccupation with time and how rapidly one can cover

a specific distance, is a preoccupation with most runners at some time in their careers. To a few however, it becomes an obsession and one meets men and women who have kept accurate running diaries of times, dates and distances for years, and they spend much of their wakeful hours thinking and training for an event time which they believe they could better. This phenomenon is generally known as *"the personal best"* and becomes a beacon of purpose towards which they strive to reach and better. For many, there is no worthier goal than to beat this tantalising time barrier even if by only a few seconds. Work, sex, food and even family become of secondary importance and the craving to achieve a new personal best becomes paramount. For these runners, the "P.B" is more important than the age category record or actually beating a well known colleague over 10 kilometres.

Occasionally, the achievement of beating one's "P.B" may have quite extreme consequences and the story of Dennis is a salutatory example. Dennis was a 64-year old runner and all his life had enjoyed both track and long distance events. Like many lifelong runners, he was of small stature and carried no excess weight on his lean, angular frame. He was of dark complexion, but his hair was now grey, receding, but always neatly parted and well trimmed. He wore rimless spectacles which inevitably steamed up after completing a run. Perhaps his most noticeable characteristic was his cultured and precise way of speaking, reflecting his background, being the product of the English public school system and Oxford University where he studied medicine in the 1950s. Not surprisingly, many found him a little aloof if not unfriendly. However, Dennis was held a little in awe for he had been a friend and training companion of Roger Bannister and had been present at the track-side on the day of the famous 4-Minute Mile.

Once a year, our local Veterans' Club held an 8-kilometre run over a flat grass course that commenced and finished with a half-loop around the local park, enabling those at the finish to watch the runners during their final 500-metre lead-up to the finishing chute and the 2 elderly ladies at the timing and record-keeping table. Dennis had enjoyed this run on several previous occasions, but for a variety of reasons, had never been able to complete it in less than 35 minutes. The previous year, he was well within the time but within a kilometre to go, his shoe-lace had come undone and he twisted his ankle and hobbled in, missing the target by a wide margin. Consequently, he had slowly been building up in his mind a preoccupation about this run for 2 years, and in the months before had put in some extra training in preparation. For the week before the run, his priority in life, his sole purpose was to be under 35 minutes and achieve a new "P.B" for this particular course.

The day of the run was cool, fresh with a clear blue sky and only a faint breeze. Most of his colleagues and fellow-runners had turned up and as usual, there was the usual atmosphere of conviviality and friendly rivalry. All he had to do was to keep, pace with several others who he knew from experience would finish in about the time he sought. A sense of purpose, goal and direction spurred him on and he felt fit and full of energy. As is sometimes the case in a run, everything seemed to come together. The breeze had strengthened and was behind him, as were several of his rival colleagues, so he sensed that he was well within his time. The grass was moist and springy under his feet and he was, as is sometimes referred to, "full of running". Finally, he entered the park and could see the finish, less than 500 metres across the oval, and less than a minute away. Thirty seconds later, the large digital figures of the timing clock came into focus and they were flashing 34 minutes and 11 seconds. Exhilarated and delighted, he knew his personal best would now be bettered after 2 years of frustration, fantasy and bad luck. Perhaps it was an old memory of Bannister breaking the 4 minutes nearly 40 years ago, or just a sense of gratification of achieving a personally constructed goal which had given his life a sense of purpose over the previous months, but he felt unusually special as his mates at the line grunted *"Well done, Dennis"* and similar utterances.

Unfortunately, his journey was not quite complete. As he jogged towards the table laden with plastic cups and cold refreshing water, he felt a strange tingling sensation in his chest and neck, and a wave of nausea swept up from the pit of his stomach. Seconds later, he cried out in anguish as a searing pain encircled his entire chest wall. He lost all sense of direction, staggered desperately towards his track-suit and towel neatly packed in an old plastic shopping bag, before collapsing into a lifeless heap on the still dew-dampened grass and to the extreme consternation of his fellow club members whose attempts at resuscitation were completely in vain.

Dennis was determined as are many other compulsive runners to achieve a sense of purpose in life by bettering his personal best, and I suspect that for most compulsive veteran runners, Dennis's mode of exit from life would be preferable to the alternative of hanging round for months or years in some cosy comfortable residential home. His persistence, determination was ultimately rewarded, but whether or not the end justified the struggle, only Dennis can judge. Or can he?

"If at first you do not succeed, try, try and try again." – old English saying.

THE SHARK CAN'T HELP IT!

It was a blustery, winter Sunday morning and one sensed an ambience of excitement and anticipation amongst the large crowd scurrying along the pavement. Even the seagulls overhead shrieked as they glided and swooped low over the bustling throng as if they were aware of some unusual occurrence. Cars, vans and motorbikes were parked a hundred metres in all directions and latecomers crawled by in low gear as they sought a suitable parking place. Beyond the road and the scrubby foreshore was the stony beach. Further still, the ocean rolled in ceaselessly from the west. Despite the blustery conditions, there was the faint yet unmistakable all-pervading smell of fish. This was not surprising as the Sunday morning crowd were responding to the large canvas advertisements in the streets informing all and sundry that there was a "huge shark" on display at Sea Roads Fish Emporium on the edge of town. Sea Roads is one of several wholesale fish outlets, where one can leisurely, browse at a large array of "Fruits de la Mer" either caught that day or frozen in giant, shiny, illuminated freezer displays. The usual dilemma for the fish lover is that of choice (if price is not a problem!). The decision is not what to buy, but which delicacy not to buy. Maybe some fresh whiting or perhaps choose the frozen King Clip and defer the succulent, mouth-watering mackerel or dhufish until the next visit.

Today, it was not possible to browse leisurely as several hundred others were milling around and forming a rough queue twenty to thirty metres long, which shuffled slowly and noisily through the double-doored entrance. Excited children escorted by apprehensive parents, young men with brightly dressed girlfriends, elderly Italian grandparents and bearded bikies all contributed to the throng. A cyclist wearing shiny shorts and a shirt covered in French slogans, carrying his helmet and pump in one hand and his camera in the other, was craning his neck in an attempt to obtain a preview.

Queues are often dreary lines of people respecting the basic democratic principles of first come, first served, but this morning the line was an interacting human chain united by excited curiosity and a sense of unifying purpose.

Passing through the double glass doors and into the central emporium, the queue led into a mass of people milling round a raised wooden platform reminiscent of a boxing ring without the rope surrounds. There, lying prostrate across the boards was the largest aquatic beast I had ever seen. It was sleek and silvery grey in colour, stretching more than five metres from tail to the tip of its nose. Even in death, it exuded the ultimate dimensions of power, ferocity and fearful omnipotence. Streamlined and shiny, slippery and strong, it lay there, imposing yet devoid of its previous strength and consciousness. Gasps and exultations of amazement, fear and disbelief were uttered by all as we gazed in awe on the beautiful shiny monster from the deep. Amazed people touched its skin nervously, others gaped in wonderment and children posed for photos in front of its massive jaws held nearly a metre agape by a wooden pole. Razor sharp, pointed teeth nearly a foot long adorned the rim of this monstrous buccal cavity. Cameras clicked and electronic flashes illuminated the surrounding displays of everyday fish which paled into insignificance by comparison. One of the men at Sea Roads told us that it had taken them two hours to catch it and two cranes were required to lift it on board. The hook embedded in its cartilaginous jaw bone was nearly a metre long and had taken two strong men over half an hour to extricate.

As we were listening to the so-called heroic details, I was

standing by its lifeless unblinking eye which seemed to stare at us with sadness and defeat. Only a few hours earlier, this superbly crafted and highly evolved visual organ which could function equally well at the surface of the ocean or in the gloom at five hundred metres below had been operating as creation had intended.

Until it bit the razor sharp hook disguised by a large lump of raw meat, the magnificent creature was minding its own business, following its daily routine and impulses as dictated by instinct and the workings of its complex central nervous system. Are we really so clever, that with our modern equipment and technology, we can suddenly interfere and smash this ancient and miraculous cycle of life?

The human psyche is predominantly irrational and it is only when we reluctantly probe its depths that we realise how much we are directed by myth and fantasy. The shark seems to represent what we fear most: an all-powerful, silent, swiftly moving monster that is always there waiting to come up from the depths and the shadows, and consume us in one large bite. Young men in powerful cars and jet fighter pilots decorate the front ends of their machines with similar archetypal mouth images. Louis Armstrong made a hit record with "Mack the Knife", film-makers, not content with their fortune from "Jaws", felt moved to complete and create "Jaws II". These manifestations of human fear are ancient, as testified by such stories as "Jonah and the Whale". To put a huge shark on display somehow reassures us that we are infallible as a species, and that we really do not have anything to fear. Psychologists sometimes refer to this mechanism as a counterphobic response. There are many other practices in addition to gloating over dead sharks. Other examples such as bunjee-jumping, rock-climbing, parachuting and speleology being but a few examples of the denial of fear and of death itself.

Whilst the validity of these explanations continues to be a matter for conjecture and debate, there is another twist to this phenomenon. As the crowds ogle and gasp in awe at the fallen monster, another crowd of humans are standing waist-deep in the ocean just a few hundred kilometres north of Sea Roads Emporium. As we take a closer look at them, they are just as excited and awed, but their exhilaration is evoked by the presence of scores of live sleek, shiny creatures whose fins and blow-holes are sticking above the surface of the water. These creatures actually seem to enjoy being stroked and petted and fussed by human beings. Dolphins, it would appear, have now acquired a reputation for being intelligent, conscious, and aware of kindness and even empathy. Not surprisingly, any suggestion of inflicting harm upon these creatures raises indignation and accusations of insensitive cruelty.

A few hundred kilometres south of our helpless shark, hundreds of volunteers have been struggling for hours in chilly seas throughout the night to assist in rescuing a group of beached killer whales which inexplicably took a wrong turn and stranded themselves upon high land only to be marooned as the tide receded. When rescue attempts fail as often they do, the human saviours are greatly distressed and can sometimes be seen on our television screens weeping with anguish and despair.

In June 1994, an intrepid skin diver attracted much public attention by appearing in a photograph on the front page of some newspapers riding on the back of a large whale in the sea off the coast of southern New South Wales. He had been snorkelling in a conventional manner when the monster mammal emerged from the depths beneath him. Being of an intrepid temperament, he turned the incident into a unique adventure and somehow managed to stand upright upon the heaving creature's back, thus bringing him temporary fame. Unfortunately, the matter was taken up by the Wildlife Protection Society who are suing him for contravening existing legislation in the Wildlife Protection Act, which prohibits swimmers from encroaching nearer the 30 metres to aquatic animals, such as whales, whilst they are in their natural environment. The maximum penalty possible is $100,000.

Why this misdirected sentimentality for some creatures and why the triumphant gloating over the demise of others? Why two sets of radically different behaviours and feelings for these not dissimilar aquatic creatures? We naively and childishly make illogical and irrational assumptions regarding the intentions of these creatures in question. It is as if we blame the shark for being the frightening creature it is, and we praise the dolphin for its wish to relate with humankind, and we feel sad for the plight of nature's abandonment of whales. This irrational and innate subjectivity towards our non-human relatives suggests that if we respond to them in this arbitrary and inconsistent manner, is it not surprising that we are also inconsistent in our dealings with those of our own kind?

Perhaps there is a link, some sort of psychological parallel between our paradoxical attitudes to these marine creatures and the gross, irrational genocidal behaviours which keep appearing in places like Cambodia, Rwanda, Bosnia and Germany. If only we could identity and correct the unconscious triggers which repeatedly plunge us back into nasty, inhuman behaviours, then perhaps we could make a further step up the precarious ladder of civilisation and away from the ever-present menacing shark-like jaws of barbarianism.

It was with these troubled thoughts that I left the Fish Emporium. As I emerged back into the sunshine and fresh air, away from the odour of fish and human hubbub, a childish hymn from Sunday School days of nearly half a century ago intruded into my perplexed consciousness, and somehow the words acquired new significance in the light of the morning's experience:

> "All things bright and beautiful
> All creatures great and small
> All things wise and wonderful
> The Lord God made them all."

Danger dwelling in the ocean

SYDNEY – Lightning kills more Australians than sharks do.

But three fatal shark attacks in six weeks have beachgoers wondering whether sharks – if not lightning – might strike twice in the same place.

Deaths from shark attacks are rare – Australia has recorded less than one a year over the past 200 years.

Even bee stings claim two or three lives a year, and lightning strikes over the past two decades have killed 19 people – seven more than sharks.

However, statistics are unlikely to allay the fears of millions about to enjoy their summer plunge around a sunny continent surrounded by water. Three deaths in such a short time represent an unusual statistical blip.

The gruesome nature of such attacks also plays on the public imagination. So does the fact that the latest attack occurred off a suburban Perth beach in full view of onlookers.

Many Australians will be asking: if it can happen there once, what's to stop it happening again?

And what's to stop it happening at my beach?

Two lives were lost in South Australian waters in the last week of September.

But there hasn't been a shark death in Victoria for three years, in NSW or Tasmania for seven years, in Queensland for eight years or in the Northern Territory for 29 years.

The last fatal attack in Sydney harbour was in 1963.

Many more people die other ways in Australia's beaches, rivers, harbours, lakes and lagoons.

Over 400 people have drowned accidentally in such locations in the past five years – including 68 swimmers, 14 divers and 13 rock anglers.

Sharks do not necessarily attack humans because they are hungry.

In fact they may not particularly relish the taste of people.

The only way for a shark to identify an animal is to bite it, experts say, pointing out that only 20 to 40 per cent of attacks on humans are fatal.

Many victims wear wet suits and may be mistaken for seals, according to Australian Shark Attack File curator John West.

Experts suggest a variety of reasons for attacks, including curiosity, territorial behaviour and disruption during breeding.

If you do spot a shark, they say, the best thing to do is to get out of the water as quickly and quietly as possible. But if an attack is imminent, any action could help – hitting the shark, gouging its eyes, making sudden movements and even blowing bubbles.

Sharks may kill up to 100 people worldwide each year.

But humans kill some 200 million sharks.

From the 'West Australian' November 2000.

51

THE SHADOW CONFRONTED
("A Fishy Tale")

"We all carry a shadow and the less it is embodied
in the individual's conscious life, the blacker and denser it is."
(Carl Jung)

Even on a fine summer's day, Moorhaven Hospital looked grey and foreboding. True, the moors behind could reflect the beauties of the Devonshire seasons with the magical gold brown tones of early autumn and with the deep purple from millions of tiny heather flowers as a backdrop. In winter, after a light dusting of snow, the first glint of sunshine would illuminate a scene of such sparkling splendour that one had to stop the car simply to gaze in awe. Despite these environmental attractions, Moorhaven Hospital could never have been anything else but a Victorian psychiatric hospital built at a time when community psychiatry was but an odd idea in a few eccentric minds to serve the whole population of South Devon. For nearly a hundred years, anyone in the county who became psychiatrically unwell (then defined as "insanity") would be committed to the large wards, the long corridors and the benevolent custodial care of mental health nurses and the Psychiatrist Superintendent. Over 400 patients resided in Moorhaven, some for years, a few for their entire lives. Throughout Britain and indeed most of the western world, hospitals such as Moorhaven were home to thousands of people with psychiatric illness.

In addition to medical and nursing staff, Moorhaven

employed hundreds of local people who worked the laundry and supervised the gardens. There were engineers, welfare officers, typists and a team of administrators led by an Administrative Superintendent. The latter met weekly with the nursing and psychiatrist Superintendents in order to discuss policy matters, planning and other household issues such as the details for the next Open Day or the Christmas menu for the patients.

It is my personal experience that asylum administrators were some of the most dull, uninspiring and humourless men in the health industry. Invariably, they wore dark suits, plain ties, grey socks, plain leather shoes and at times would appear almost zombie-like. Maybe it was because of the nature of their duties but they smiled little, they would only speak if you spoke to them first, and would usually avoid your gaze as you walked down the long, cold, green-painted corridors of asylums. Of course, there were exceptions, but generally, this mournful corpus of administrators did little to embellish or put a spark into one's dreary day within these grey sombre buildings.

I often wondered what went on in their private lives and in their conscious thoughts. This was of passing interest at the time for as a junior trainee doctor studying and reading for specialist exams, one was taught that the characteristics observed in an individual were but a superficial veneer serving to conceal elements which are the opposite to what we observe and believe to be the true nature of the person. To quote Jung: "Unfortunately there can be no doubt that man is on the whole less good than he imagines himself or wants to be. Everyone carries a shadow. We carry our past with us, to wit. the primitive and inferior man with his desires and emotions, and it is only with an enormous effort that we can detach ourselves from this burden." According to Jung, the reconciliation and balance between these opposites is one of the major functions of both the individual psyche and of civilization itself.

It was thus with curiosity and interest that I accepted an invitation to go conger eel fishing one Friday night in October after work. My curiosity was evoked because my previous experience of eels had been in the warm waters of the Bahamas where, as an amateur skin-diver, one is taught religiously to avoid approaching the gaping fangs of the Moray eel quivering with unblinking eyes, guarding the entrance to his small underwater cave. Stories are told of the ferocious bite of powerful jaws and the eel's reluctance to release its hold of the unwary diver's arm or leg. However, because my invitation was from the Hospital's Finance Officer and most of the administrative staff were going, I was fascinated as to what sort of glum adventure I was destined for. Fred Crooke (the Pensions Clerk) was a small man who wore National Health Service wire-framed spectacles that always seemed too large and tended to slip down his nose. He wore the same grey tie every day and one of those striped shirts with a plain white collar that appeared as if it was attached separately. His black hair was kept short and brushed back in what was almost a crew cut. His breast pocket was always adorned by a white handkerchief which he frequently kept pulling out and stuffing back in again during conversation. He seemed to have overall charge of the adventure and told me in a serious voice that Plymouth Sound was perishing cold at night and I would be well advised to put on plenty of clothes. He was right. Peter Booth, the Hospital Secretary, was probably the most extroverted of this little band of administrative men, and as he lived in the next village of South Brent, he kindly agreed to pick me up and drive to the waiting-boat. By 7.00 o'clock we had parked, donned several layers of clothes and an extra pair of trousers. I also sported a woollen balaclava and Wellington boots.

The old wooden fishing-boat was moored by the Barbican Steps. As we approached, the diesel engine was already chugging away and pouring out blue smoke into the chilly evening air, illuminated by a large single lamp at the top of the mast. There were ten of us, and an ambience of mild expectation and excitement prevailed as the wooden craft throbbed out into the October evening and choppy waters of the Sound. The weather was damp, but fortunately the drizzle of the earlier evening had cleared, leaving behind a thin molecular film of moisture over everything, giving a feeling of intense cold and damp. I then noticed I was the only member of the party wearing Wellingtons, my companions all wearing large industrial leather boots. Harry Grindle, the Canteen Officer, had tied his trousers around the top of his boots with white sisal finished off with two large ugly knots.

The elderly vessel creaked and chugged into the Sound. Harry provided me with a large reel of nylon fishing line on the end of which were 3 or 4 steel hooks, and nearer the end a couple of large lead weights were attached. At the foot of the mast, was a large plastic bucket full of putrid raw fish conveniently chopped up into chunks which we fixed onto the hooks as bait. The smell was quite disagreeable and the fingers turned blue with cold. Lines were cast overboard and played out until the reel was nearly empty. George, the hospital gardener, now our helmsman, directed the boat in slow motion and we trawled in large sweeping circles in the vicinity of the ancient breakwater. In the far distance, the street lamps of Plymouth twinkled and the slow-moving lights of motorcars filtered through the misty gloom as they crossed the Tamar bridge.

As we waited in patient expectation, I nervously confessed that I knew absolutely nothing about conger eels, and that I would have no idea what to do if I was fortunate enough to hook one. Furthermore, I explained I had no idea what conger eels looked like, how big they were or even whether they were edible or not. This admission and my obvious apprehension caused a ripple of mirth around the boat, and I became aware of some unique Devonshire phrases which I had not previously heard: *"Arr, just eee wait a bit!"* laughed a tall thin man whom I recognized as the hospital engineer. *"Ee won't be disappointed."* I sensed an aura of increasing excitement and expectancy, something bigger than I had anticipated seemed not far off. I tugged on the taut line, but to my inexperienced hand, it did not seem different to a couple of minutes before. I was contemplating winding it in when Fred Crooke suddenly shouted out in great excitement: *"I have ee! I have ee!"* he cried. All eyes turned towards Fred who was in the bow of the boat, feverishly winding in his line into spiralled tangles on the deck floor. *"Pull it in, Fred!"* someone shouted, and Fred complied by dragging over the side one of the most evil disagreeable beasts I had ever seen. The conger eel was over a metre in length. It was slimy, green, writhing and flapping on the woodwork of the boat-floor. The single light swinging from the mast reflected upon its dark green scaly skin and its pink eyes flashed in the murky light. Its large flat tail thrashed about frighteningly, but the most sinister end was its head and large jaw snapping and chomping on the half-swallowed steel baited hook.

At this point, the collective shadow of my usually reserved administrative colleagues was released! Pandemonium! Several large men simultaneously tried to control it by jumping on it. Others attempted to hold it still whilst someone else hit it on the head with a large lump of wood and attempted to wrench the barbed hook from the snapping awesome jaws. Now I know why they were wearing large boots. Apart from one young man who I think was an Assistant Clerk who attempted to climb up the mast, there had been an instant personality change. It was as if this slimy monster symbolized the archetypal creatures within the human psyche which evoked this great release of savage energy. Within 5 minutes, the primeval conger from the icy depths of Plymouth Sound had thrashed out its last futile attempts to escape and there was a sense of relief and victory as the crew returned again to their own lines. During the next two and half hours, 4 more of these primitive leviathans were dragged out from the murky depths, and the entire performance was repeated until they were all overpowered by the crew of heavily-booted men, cursing and swearing in thick West Country accents, only partially understandable to the outsider.

It was quite late as we tied up near Mayflower steps. The air was cold, damp and misty, quite the opposite to the spirits of my colleagues who were cheerful and victorious as all around our feet lay the slimy corpses, still occasionally flapping and writhing, of the primitive monsters of which we are usually unaware but are ever-present in murky depths beneath the superficially busy waters of Plymouth Sound.

There is a sad finale to this fisherman's yarn, for the following morning, my wife (on my insistence) captured the victory on film as I held aloft the metre-long prize from the previous night's activities. As is sometimes the case, the film remained inside the camera for several months before some other significant family event required recording for posterity. Unfortunately, it was only after processing that it was discovered that the conger eel's image was on the last frame, and I had been neatly sliced off from the neck down, effectively denying the true nature of my heroism and the true enormity of the behemoth from the gloomy depths of Plymouth Sound.

Footnote: Moorhaven Hospital closed in 1985 and has since been refurbished, decorated and internally restructured into desirable accommodation on the edge of Dartmoor so City workers can retreat from the pressures of everyday urban living.

DEATH, REBIRTH AND DECEPTION

The American sociologist and writer, Ernest Becker, maintained that Sigmund Freud's psychoanalytical theory was basically wrong. It is not the suppression of sexual instincts and drives which are responsible for the neurotic miseries of human kind but the constant denial of our personal mortality. I read his book, "The denial of death", a few years ago and whilst accepting the credibility of his hypothesis never gave it much thought until a small light brown fury creature entered our family.

Ralph was no ordinary hamster but that was not surprising. He had been selected by my young son from a large metal cage at the local pet shop. This comprised an enclosure containing hundreds of other little fury creatures twisting and seething apparently randomly apart from a few that were intent on drinking water or seizing a food pellet from a central plastic feeding station. Ralph was special not only because he was now our hamster but because his residence was utterly different to the earlier pandemonium that he had experienced.

He now lived in a purpose-built unit constructed in conventional western style and had adapted remarkably well to these new quarters. Downstairs was a six inch rotating wheel which he had soon learnt to operate by climbing inside and setting into motion by frantically running on the spot for minutes on end and then resting a short while as the wheel rocked like a pendulum coming to rest before commencing on another apparently goalless journey. He would then dismount, sniff furtively and scamper to the plastic dispenser and help himself to water, cheese, mixed nuts or nibble at a fresh lettuce leaf.

He then ascended from the downstairs activity area up into the bathroom and sleeping quarters. The bath was a small tin lid filled with fresh water and the bedroom a separate compartment into which fresh straw had been layed. There seemed no doubt that Ralph enjoyed his sleeping area for not only did he spend much time curled up luxuriously in the straw, he also had the annoying habit of dragging lumps of cheese or half lettuce leaves upstairs through the door where he could consume them at leisure. No strategies were ever discovered to persuade him to use the especially constructed toilet area in the downstairs rear left quarter. Whilst this existence was rather special for a hamster what really enhanced the whole affair was that the entire wall of the residence consisted of a large vertical piece of glass cleverly set into lateral slots enabling it to be raised up and down for cleaning, maintenance and general access purposes. This enabled my son and his friends the opportunity to observe Ralph in all his routines whenever they wished. In addition to these superb viewing facilities his dining quarters were enhanced by a small electric torch bulb set in a socket in the dining room area roof which could be turned on from a bicycle battery and switch.

Within a couple of days Ralph had not only adjusted to suburban life, he had also become quite friendly and when the large glass front was elevated, would run down the stairs, sniff the air for a couple of seconds and then walk nervously onto the outstretched hand of the gleeful child. Unfortunately, as sometimes occurs, all good things come to a premature end. So it was with Ralph. It was a Saturday lunchtime and the family were preparing to eat. The table was set and my wife was serving up portions onto waiting plates. My son was in the room interacting with Ralph and the distant whirring of the treadmill was evidence of ongoing activity. As the plates were duly moved into their positions on the table the familiar utterance "lunch is ready" was called and we sat down awaiting our son's arrival. A few seconds later he had not arrived but before he was hailed again a shrill plaintive cry of despair reached our ears. Within seconds I was in his room witnessing the cause of his distress. Ralph's small frame was trapped under the sharp cutting edge of the plate glass as it guillotined down on his tiny fragile neck. Catastrophe! I looked with horror at the scene. Ralph was experiencing his last few seconds of hamster consciousness and was slipping into the eternal void. His dark blinking eye looked pleadingly upwards. A small shining red bead of blood trickled down his tiny nostril. He had been effectively and incisively executed as he sought nothing more than one last friendly scratch on his bristly nose. I was reminded of an eccentric colleague who I worked with in France many years ago who sought permission to attempt communication with those guillotined to test the validity of the belief that the brain remains conscious for at least 30 seconds following the cessation of oxygen. Two more opposing thoughts then intruded. First the importance of being truthful with young children about death and dying and second the importance of avoiding guilt in my sons mind as it was his little hand that released the heavy glass resulting in the unfortunate execution.

In retrospect one never knows how or why a particular course of action commences in a crisis. There were two alternatives, one was to pronounce death there and then and deal with the consequences or secondly to practice some form of deceitful slight of hand. I suspect that it is in response to crisis the true personality becomes manifest for I took the second more cowardly option.

After reassuring him everything was in order I despatched him to the dining room for his lunch and carefully lifted the lethal sheet of glass and removed the limp warm little creature from his own front door. I carried him quietly through the hall and into the kitchen where I cosily wrapped him in aluminium foil making sure that both ends of the resulting sausage was securely sealed. In semi-automatic mode I picked up the motor car keys and announced to the seated family that Ralph had injured his neck and I was taking him to the vet for immediate attention.

I drove around the block three times wondering just what was the best coarse of action for Ralph now inert and entombed in aluminium foil on the passenger seat beside me. I opened the glove box and popped him inside. As it clicked the courtesy light seemed almost pleased to turn itself off. I returned home, took my lunch out of the oven and informed the family that the vet had decided to "keep him in for 24 hours". The fragile ambience of calm was thus maintained. There was no inquiry, no more questions and the household affairs resumed to normal save for the absence of the familiar noise of the whirring treadmill wheel. The following day I returned to the pet shop with the precious aluminium bundle clasped in my hand and sought the timid young man who had sold us Ralph just a week ago and stood nearby whilst he completed a sale of two small fish in a plastic bag. As he turned to serve me I politely offered him the small parcel "I'm afraid this hamster that I bought last week is dead" I mournfully explained, "Would you like to see it?". He stepped backwards and gasped. His dark face seemed to pale a little "No man" he expostulated "Throw it in the bin and get another".

I never thought it would be so easy! The most difficult task was to find a suitable Ralph look-alike for although there were hundreds of little beasts scurrying, leaping, eating or just preening themselves, they were all different in their markings and colour and even, I thought, their facial expression. Finally I picked up a rather docile little specimen in the corner of the cage and took him home in an air-holed disposable cardboard container kindly supplied by the pet shop.

My son was delighted as I returned triumphant and Ralph (number 2) was introduced into the hamster home (now with modified safety features). Rightly or wrongly guilt had been avoided and the denial of mortality had been circumvented despite the ancient cycle of death and rebirth being reinacted in our very own home.

Ralph 2 soon became familiar with the luxuries of hamster mansion and like his predecessor insisted not only in taking food upstairs into his bedroom but refused to use the downstairs toilet area preferring once more the privacy of his bedroom, a most unsavoury practice. For some unexplainable reason Ralph number 2 could never be persuaded to use the treadmill, even if placed directly in it with a tasty lump of cheese a few inches in front of him. He would anxiously jump off, rush into a corner and wash his face. Despite this it was not for many years that the truth about Ralph was finally revealed. His reluctance to use the wheel was explained as being due to dizziness following his neck injury and eventually it was removed and replaced by a small mirror in front of which he would occasionally gaze in apparent perplexity. Sometimes I suspect honest deception is less traumatic than the pain of truth but perhaps that is the rationalisation of a coward.

RESURRECTION OR RESUSCITATION

But, if for instance the statement that Christ rose from the dead is to be under stood not literally but symbolically, then it is capable of various interpretations that do not conflict with knowledge and do not impair the meaning of the statement. The objection that understanding it symbolically puts an end to the Christian hope of immortality is invalid, because long before the coming of Christianity mankind believed in a life after death and therefore had no need of the Easter event as a guar antee of immortality. The danger that a mythology understood too literally, and as taught by the church will suddenly be repudiated lock, stock and barrel is today greater than ever. Is it not time that the Christian mythology, instead of being wiped out was understood symbolically for once?

Carl Jung. The Undiscovered Self. Collected works vol 10 (19560 P.266)

It was a cold damp morning and the sun had not yet climbed high enough to cast shadows inside the small low-ceilinged square room. The walls were made of large white limestone blocks which fitted neatly together, obviously assembled by skilled craftsmen builders. On one end of this rather featureless enclosure, was a rectangular door space across which hung a brightly coloured fabric. On the opposing walls two square glassless windows opened to the grey morning sky beyond.

The air, although still, was heavy with the sweet smells of aromatic oils and healing linaments contained in a variety large terracotta pots standing along the wall. The floor was the earth itself, trodden flat by thousands of sandalled feet over many years. Brightly coloured woven straw-mats lay on the floor, but the intricate design was hidden by four apprehensive people sitting cross-legged in the approaching dawn. The four of them, two men and two women, were dressed in long white Eastern-style robes around which their fatigued bodies protected them from the chill of the previous night as their vigil had commenced late on the previous afternoon. The heads of the ill-shaven and gaunt-looking men were enveloped in coloured turbans whilst the women wore large cloth shawls covering all but their anxious faces. In the centre of this small room lay the focus of their gaze, the cause of their predicament.

On a raised pallet of straw covered by a fine-woven blanket, was the body of a frail-looking man seemingly much older than his 34 years. His skin was pale and ashen, around his forehead and temples were angry-looking healing scars, his long hair lay loosely to one side of his head and his unkempt beard fell onto the thin sheet covering his chest which for several hours had risen and fallen erratically, being the only sign that the otherwise immobile body possessed of that mysterious phenomenon we know as *"life"*.

The silence of the room was occasionally broken by brief interchanges between the four onlookers who had spent the long night gently bathing his battered, dehydrated body, cleaning his wounds, applying healing ointments and salves to his punctured skin. As they laboured, they muttered prayers to God that he might eventually survive the horrors of the previous day's ordeal.

Outside, the sky began to brighten and in the distance was the faint bleating of sheep grazing on the nearby hillside. A few seconds later, the strident crowing of a nearby cockerel disturbed the weary reveries of the small group. Suddenly, the prostrate figure on the straw pallet coughed, turned his head and began to moan in a semi-delirious state. As he slowly drifted back to consciousness and self-awareness, his wife (the youngest of the four) attempted to rise to his aid, but was held back by the older woman who bade her wait a while. It was with amazement and relief that they watched as he slowly returned to wakefulness and began to explore the injuries on his hands and wrists only to recoil in pain as he touched the still ruptured gashes in his skin. The younger woman could be restrained no longer. She leapt to her feet and with a clean cloth dipped into one of the pots, rushed to his side where she knelt and commenced to gently caress his pale and furrowed brow.

Within minutes, she was able to drip cool water from the nearby jug into his parched mouth and although still distressed and in pain, the man was able to recognise and mutter thanks to his friends who had so diligently and at risk to their own safety, rescued and nursed him back to a state where recovery, convalescence and further life was now possible.

Over the next two days, signs of health returned rapidly as his companions continued to lavish loving care, facilitating his speedy rehabilitation. His wife, assisted by his elderly mother cleaned and dressed the wounds with aloe vera, myrrh and palm leaves twice a day, and washed his body with cool sweetly scented warm water, and provided him with clean fresh linen. The two male companions brought in goat's milk, cheese, fruit and local red wine. On the second day, they helped him to his feet, supporting him as he took his first faltering steps.

By the third day, his strength had returned and a sense of impatience and boredom began to complicate his predicament, causing concern to his carers, as Jesus (whom the reader will by now have recognised) was assumed by both Romans and the Jewish hierarchy to be dead; out of the way and no longer a threat and embarrassment to social order. The previous Friday, Pontius Pilate had reluctantly agreed to his crucifixion late in the afternoon, his usual cautious decision-making style having been swayed not just by the persuasive arguments of the Jewish accusers, but also because it was the beginning of a long week-end festival and public holiday. Consequently, as Jesus's mental and physical faculties ebbed back into his being, he was not fully aware of the grave danger he was in if the authorities discovered that he been unofficially removed from the cross before the cessation of his vital functions.

His friends' concerns were augmented the following day when early in the morning whilst they slept, Jesus took a stroll on the dusty track that led to the village of Ennaus. Despite the earliness of the day, he met a group of old friends who, still in a state of shock and mourning, initially failed to recognise him. On returning to the house, his friends were alarmed to hear of this encounter, for if the news reached the ears of either the Roman or Jewish authorities, they could have been arrested and charged with interfering with the process of law. The authorities were already unhappy that Jesus (presumed to be dead) had been taken to the tomb of a private citizen, rather than placed, as was the custom, into a communal grave. So, fearful of these consequences, the only escape was for him to go into hiding, away from his enemies and persecutors, to some place where there was a sympathetic established Jewish community who were unaware of the political tensions and conflicts that had developed over the previous weeks in Israel.

SANCTUARY, SAFETY AND ASYLUM
What happened next will forever remain unclear as the various accounts differ. The conventional Christian story is that a few days later, he went with friends onto a mountain top and disappeared or ascended into heaven, never to be seen again. Whilst this legend was very persuasive in converting misbelievers to Christianity, it was also convenient in leading others to conclude that not only he was dead but also a supernatural being who had come to earth on a special mission to save the human race from sin and self-destruction.

More recently, biblical scholars reviewing evidence from ancient scrolls and writings believe his friends took him to a monastery until the hue and cry died down, where he lived a reclusive life with his wife and children before dying in the city of Ephesus at the age of 73. Other scholars believe that Jesus and his family went into exile in the south of France where there was an established Jewish community. A hypothesis supported by a body of evidence that Jesus and his family were the originators of the Merovian blood line and a dynasty traceable today through King Dagobert. It is recorded that Dagobert married a Gisele de Rases in 671 and that Razes (a Roman fort at the time) was later renamed Rennes le Chateau where in 1886 the local priest discovered some ancient coded parchments whose analysis and deciphering implied that the body of Christ was buried secretly in the vicinity. The priest subsequently became extremely wealthy and many have speculated that he was "paid off" by the Catholic church to keep silent about his discovery. Other writers assert that Jesus changed his name and left Israel to continue his ministry in Kashmir where he eventually died and was buried in Syrinigar. There is also a legend that Jesus visited Glastonbury early in the 1st century but the evidence is less convincing.

The Australian theological scholar Barbara Thiering has written several books on her interpretations of the New Testament, The Thomas Gospel and the dead sea scrolls using a code she calls the "Pescher" method to uncover the hidden meanings. After years of meticulous detective work she concludes that like many others who were crucified Jesus did not die at the crucifixion and for the next 40 years was a central figure in a political movement to overthrow the Pagan Roman Empire. She also believes that Jesus had two sons, who played an important in the evolution of this underground religious movement which was growing out of Judaism. The base of this movement was Ephesus where (she claims) Jesus died in A.D.70

The story so far is of course fiction based on the assumption that Jesus was resuscitated from unconsciousness rather than resurrected from death following crucifixion. In view of recent archaeological findings and writings, the conventional Christian version which has prevailed for over 2,000 years is becoming less plausible and more like a contrived fiction constructed by early church leaders to persuade the heathen and pagans to accept Christianity as the only true faith. Historians tell us that the cross and the crucifixion did not become symbols of Christianity until the Xth century and were not even depicted at all until the early VIIth century. These are intriguing hypotheses and there is no shortage of literature for those interested and enjoy historical speculation. However, none of this speculation about Christ's post crucifixion life could be relevant if he had died.

Every year, as Easter approaches, we are bombarded by the annual razzamatazz of fluffy chickens, chocolate eggs and advertisements for St Matthew's passion. The origins of this festival are pagan, but it is not clear just how ancient it is. Scholars inform us that it originated from the Anglo-Saxon name "Eastre" which refers to the Teutonic goddess of spring, fertility and rebirth, but was then adopted by the early Christian church about 340 A.D. to encourage non-believers to join in the anniversary rituals of the crucifixion.

With the passage of time, the earlier origins of Easter have been forgotten and millions of children continue to be indoctrinated with the unquestioning belief that Easter with all the chicken and egg rituals is a Christian phenomenon. This is not the case!

To question the supernatural explanation that Jesus was resurrected is thought by many to be heretical, but there is adequate and increasing evidence to believe that he was taken down from the cross before death and resuscitated either by close friends or colleagues at the Essene monastery, where he had known associations.

In 1863, a French writer called Renan created a storm with the publication of a book entitled *"The Life of Jesus"*. This disputed the divinity and supernatural image of Jesus and described him as a *"magnetic teacher with a vivid personality and being an incomparable man"*. Renan noted that according to the gospels, the crucifixion took place around noon and Jesus's apparent death occurred suddenly about 3.00 p.m when he was taken down and laid in a tomb, but at dawn on Sunday (40 hours later), was no longer there. Renan (who studied and researched his book in the Holy Land) also noted that recovery after crucifixion was a well-known phenomenon at the time.

Albert Schweitzer, the famous Belgian scholar, musician and Christian missionary wrote his famous controversial book *"The Quest of Historical Jesus"* which again disputed the mystical, supernatural picture of Jesus and made a plea for an *"objective study of Christian origins"*.

In 1908, an article appeared in the New York *"Medical Record"* expressing the view that Jesus's apparent death could be explained by a fainting attack caused by a fall in blood pressure due to immobilisation in the upright position. This theory was followed up in 1935 by Professor S Weiss, an American authority on fainting, who believed that fainting preceded death in victims of crucifixion, which is why it was common practice to break the victim's legs in order to ensure the certainty of death. As we know from the Scriptures, Jesus's legs were not broken in the usual manner.

In 1960, Dr J G Bourne, an anaesthetist in Salisbury was investigating the physiological mechanisms of fainting under general anaesthetics in the dentist's chair. He suggested that to minimize the risks associated with prolonged fainting (which included death), it was much safer to have the patient in a horizontal position during dental procedures, which as most of us have experienced, is now standard practice. Dr Bourne's observations led him to compare the similarities between crucifixion and fainting.

In fainting, blood pressure falls precipitously, diminishing the brain's oxygen supply. Consciousness is lost and the person falls down; breathing becomes shallow, the pupils dilate and the appearance is quite death-like. Recovery from this death-like state usually occurs when the victim is laid flat or even in a head-down position, allowing gravity to ensure a return of blood to the brain.

Anaesthetic observations in the days of giving dental anaesthetics in a sitting position demonstrated that many patients collapsed, giving the appearance of death, but when they were laid flat, consciousness would return. Some within an hour, others several hours later, and rarely after a couple of days. Sadly, a few failed to recover and died.

Today, despite the sophistication of medical technology, people are occasionally pronounced dead (sometimes in hospital) and are transported to the local mortuary where they are later discovered by astonished staff to be alive, once again demonstrating that the diagnosis of death is not always straightforward, and that even medical experts can be mistaken.

Increasing doubt over the validity of the Resurrection comes not only from new archaeological and physiological evidence, but also from within the Church itself. In 1999, the Archbishop of Canterbury stated *"there is now enough historical evidence to prove beyond reasonable doubt that Jesus lived, however there is not the same amount of evidence that he was resurrected."*

It is not surprising that close friends and relatives failed to recognise Jesus as not only did they assume he was dead, he would have looked ill and wasted after his ordeal. He may well have suffered temporary minor brain damage as a result of lack of oxygen and his speech may have been a little slurred and his mental processes and memory impaired.

Such is the uncertainty of diagnosing death that a few years ago in the early days of organ transplant surgery, there were accusations (and a television documentary) of hearts and kidneys being removed before the donor was dead. This resulted in the medical profession inventing a new definition of **"brain death"** in which electrical brain activity must be absent for a specified period of time.

There are many who ask *"why it is important and what difference does it make if the Resurrection is a contrived myth?"*.

There are two principal responses. First, for scores of generations, millions of children have been indoctrinated with the misleading crucifixion story, the Resurrection, large stones being miraculously moved, angels standing in a tomb and subsequent ascension from the top of a mountain up into the sky. While some may claim the reason for this story was originally well-intentioned, it was based on deceit, dishonesty and dogma, thus denying generations of people the choice of drawing their own conclusions without bias or coercion. Second, in todays complex and technical world the emphasis is on logical, analytical and propositional thinking and any suggestion of meta-physical or supernatural explanation for doctrines which contain dogmatic assertions in reaching conclusions are regarded with scepticism and doubt. In the modern world knowledge and belief is based on evidence based comclusions and not on unquestioned leaps of faith. Consequently life after death, reincarnation and resurrection are for many quite unacceptable theories for explaining survival after crucifixion, existence or the meaning of life.

The increasing interest in Buddhism and other eastern religions is an example of the rejection of this style of thinking which Jung referred to as archaic. The Buddha, despite his wisdom and profound teachings, many of which were mirrored 600 years later by Jesus, died at a ripe old age from cholera, never claimed that he was other than mortal! Interestingly there is some evidence that Jesus attended a Buddhist Monastery in Alexandria during his families exile in Egypt. There is little doubt that Jesus lived and was known for his wisdom, his charismatic style of teaching, his "magnetic" personality and for his remarkable insights into the human psyche.

If the elders of the present day church could consider the not unreasonable hypothesis that his survival was due to resuscitation rather than resurrection then many Christian sceptics might find Christianity more acceptable and return to the church which they currently view as medieval and with feelings of alienation. Don Cupitt, theologian and writer wrote in his popular book, *"The Sea of Faith"* that *"We live in a time when old religious certainties are dissolving away, but this is no matter for lament, for it is the nature of all certainties so to dissolve"* Our notion of God can never be any thing else than metaphoric. *"People have been struggling for too long to hold onto a meaning of God which is passing away, no doubt because they think that this meaning is THE meaning, the only possible meaning. But if meanings change and must be re-minted then we should be looking for signs of a profound mutation of Christianity; a reforging of all its meanings"* The era of metaphysics and belief in the supernatural is past. Today the metaphor of resuscitation is more apposite as a description of the wondrous natural cycle of birth, life and rebirth than the magical notion of resurrection.

No one would doubt that in todays world of material abundance, unchecked consumerism and spiritual poverty an acceptable and meaningful faith is urgently required. The teachings of Jesus are relevant to todays multiple dilemmas but unless the elders of the Christian church are willing to relinquish some of their power, become more flexible and shed some out-dated and magical concepts increasing numbers of intelligent people will continue to find it an unacceptable doctrine.

"Irrationally held truths may be more harmful
than reasoned errors."
(T.H. Huxley 1881)

The Thin Line of Life

It was a fresh golden autumn morning as we drove to work over the high fields of the Southern Peak district. In the far distance was Chatsworth house, grand and magnificent, surrounded on all sides by the rich multi-coloured forests and meadows sparkling and glinting as the early morning sun reflected and refracted from millions of droplets of water from the previous evening's rain.

Suddenly, without warning, a beautiful cock pheasant strode proudly from the hedge only a few metres ahead. He was quite oblivious and completely unaware of our speeding car which an instant later crushed him to death. We cringed in horror at the sound of the soft yet lethal thud as his neck went under our wheel. The misshapened pile of crumpled feathers in the rear view mirror confirmed the end of yet another miracle of the phenomenon we refer to as life. Fortunately, we only occasionally reflect on the fragility, the precariousness and the temporariness of life. I say fortunately, because if we were not possessed with the mental mechanisms of denial, dissociation and repression, the close proximity of Thanatos would make life unbearable. Like the pheasant, when the end comes, it is preferable not to have any warning and it is troublesome to the mind to have experienced a near miss, for such an event temporarily destroys our defences. Furthermore, a near miss may well reactivate previous "narrow shaves" which although disagreeable and frightening at the time, have been buried in our ancient memory banks. So it was that the poor pheasant's premature demise, evoked recall of a previous event.

73

A warm wind blew in from the Arabian Sea and overhead the tall graceful palms bent in response. The noise of flapping leaves blended harmoniously with the hum of conversation, tinkling cutlery and the faint sound of background music. My wife and I were sitting at a candle lit table in an outdoor hotel restaurant reflecting on the day's excursions. The hotel was built on a small cliff, so the sound of waves was projected up from the beach 20 feet below. Above us were the tall palms whilst behind was the bustling activity of waiters as they scurried to and fro, balancing large trays of succulent fish curries, fresh fruit and bottles of King Fisher beer. To our right, rose a high headland on the end of which stood a red and white striped lighthouse whose thin beam scanned us all briefly every minute as it rotated on its axis. There was an ambience of cordiality and relaxation as we all sat at our little tables eating, talking, drinking, listening to the background music, soaking in the mixed sensations of warmth, wind, moonlight, exotic smells from hidden night-scented plants, the faint aroma of Indian cooking and all the thousands of other unidentifiable tropical subliminal sensations inducing a sensation of profound pleasure and well-being.

We had just finished a splendid meal of curried fish, followed by a sweet, fleshy fresh melon and was about to pour some delectably fresh smelling coffee from a large elegant pot. Then it happened. Suddenly, without warning, there was an overwhelming explosion of noise as every other sensation in which we had been basking was eliminated by an enormous crashing sound. An overwhelming experience of finality and confusion drowned out all other perception and every object on the table bounced into the air only to crash down again, spewing hot coffee in all directions. Cutlery was strewn over the surrounding grass and pieces of broken crockery were scattered everywhere.

After a few long seconds of silence, confusion broke out. Fellow diners rushed to our table, others just sat in amazement and fear. A couple of waiters ran over to investigate and to console. It is in such acute situations that seconds somehow stretch into minutes and in what seemed like a minute, my presence of mind returned and I noticed that the table, previously covered by a white linen cloth, was made of metal and the top was now bent inwards at an angle of about 45°. As hot coffee trickled off the edge like a murky brown waterfall, I saw the cause of our disquiet on the grass by my feet: a very large, heavy ripe coconut. This monster from the sky had been sitting in the swinging palms 50 feet above our heads and had gradually been loosened as its fibrous stalk became frayed by the warm gusty evening winds until the last thread snapped, releasing it to plummet down with terrifying force into the peaceful calm in the centre of our gourmet table.

The noise, the joking, the laughter and the conversation that followed for the next two hours were predictable. The management did their best to dispel fear amongst the remaining clients as other vulnerable tables were moved as a precaution, from beneath the swaying palm trees. The manager apologised and reassured us that the boy who was responsible for felling the nuts would be severely reprimanded the following day for not having done his job properly. The offending monster coconut was taken away and ceremoniously returned in two halves with the contents augmented with expensive Indian brandy. With much light-hearted jocularity, these were passed around as a sort of ritualised thanksgiving. We were given a new table (well away from the swinging palms) and a fresh pot of coffee and an extra sweet were provided.

It is sometimes said that life in India is cheap. Whether or not this is the case must be left to conjecture, but as we paid our bill the following morning the still apologetic proprietor told us that in Kerala there is a well- known saying to the effect that "in Kerala, coconuts never kill anyone". This comment has caused us much subsequent reflection and ruminating. If the large missile from above had fallen a few inches in the "other direction", then... If the wind had blown just a bit harder... If the table had been set a couple of feet to the left or right...

Later, as we were leaving, an elderly, sagacious-looking man with a shaved head reminded us that the Buddha taught there are only two certainties in life: death is unavoidable but secondly (and even more disquieting), we have no idea when it will be. Not surprisingly, we did not find these words very consoling!

This incident was without doubt a major "near miss" of alarming magnitude and for some time, I was very much aware of the fragile nature and proximity of mortality. This awareness is sometimes kindled into consciousness when the life of an innocent creature such as the pheasant is suddenly and without warning extinguished. The manager's reassurances were uttered in kindness and meant to be comforting and reassuring but is less objective than the old French dictum which states:

"Une minute avant de mourir, on est en vie!"
(A minute before you are dead, you are alive!)

FIRE DANCER

It was a still, warm tropical Balinese night. Overhead, the sky was cloudless as thousands of stars beamed down with a brightness that is never equalled in the north even on the coldest, clear frosty evening. The stillness of the night was broken by the shrill tympanic sounds of cicadas as they identified their territories, the bark of distant dogs and the expectant hubbub of curious voices.

Exotic smells of tropical flowers mingled with the mouth-watering odours of fried rice and spices. Along with another few score curious visitors, we were waiting for the evening performance to commence, seated around an old market-style square. At one end, was a bamboo-thatched roof under which were an assorted group of Balinese people including a small Gamelan orchestra, some official-looking people wearing white robes and turban-like hats. Several half-dressed young children were running around excitedly, accompanied by a few chickens and a mangy dog.

A few minutes later, one of the Gamelan gongs began to chime softly and was soon joined every few seconds until within a minute or so, the unique magical haunting sounds of Indonesia filled the air and diverted our attention away from previous thoughts and conversations. As the tingling sounds infiltrated and demanded our attention, a thin, scrawny man half-ran, half danced into the centre of the enclosure carrying a flaming bamboo torch which he thrust into a metre-high pile of coconut husks which had been previously assembled.

Within minutes, there was an incandescent burning inferno hurling sparks and wispy smoke high into the air. The heat

77

from the pyre was such that reflexedly we shaded our eyes with our hands whilst those sitting on the floor at the front shuffled backwards towards those of us who had arrived earlier and were fortunate to have found some rather unstable yet not uncomfortable rattan chairs.

Soon the melodic strains of the Gamelan were augmented by the pulsating throb of a large circular drum. This was played by a large Balinese man, naked except for a loin cloth, the drum being placed on the floor and somehow encircled by his brown shoeless spindly legs. The drumming intensified and became intrusively overwhelming and an aura of great expectancy filled the evening air. I was aware of the heat of the fire and felt the sweat running down my chest.

Suddenly, from inside the covered end of the arena, a thin, wild-looking man wearing only a red loin cloth, rushed out. His eyes were red and fixed at infinity as he gyrated in a large circle between us and the red, hot husks. The hypnotic, almost overwhelming amalgam of drum and Gamelan added to the electrifying, tense ambiance. After circling the fire a couple of times, the whirling human form then ran straight at the flaming pile and purposely kicked it over. There was a flurry of hot sparks and smoke as the glowing pieces spread out over several square metres. On-lookers gasped incredulously and fearfully in amazement as he proceeded to leap about, twisting and cavorting amongst the red-hot embers. The Balinese on lookers were also excited and leaping around the perimeter, shouting and screaming wild encouragement.

The dancer then changed his routine and ran the full diameter of the arena, through the centre of the inferno and straight to where we were sitting. His red eyes, still fixed at infinity seemed to look straight through us. Sweat was pouring from his bare chest and face as he stopped abruptly when he was but a couple of metres from us, only to then turn around and charge back through the heated centre to the other side. He repeated this performance three or four times. Then, as quickly as he began, it was over. The whole performance must have lasted about six minutes and as he collapsed, panting and breathless onto a waiting bed of straw, his accomplices poured fruit juices into his parched mouth and wiped his sweaty body with damp white cloths. After a few seconds required to recover from our dumbfounded shock, we gasped and cheered in amazement.

The drumming stopped and the Gamelan tinkled away into silence. In company with several others, I rushed to where the half-naked man lay, half-afraid as to what I might find. Then, yielding to the reflexes of years of medical practice, my fingers sought out the pulse at his wrist. It was rapid yet full, regular and bounding. Relieved to find his vital functions were intact, I looked carefully at his feet. The thick, horny skin was black, filthy and hot. Horny calluses were present under his toes but nowhere was there any blistering or evidence of burning.

Many have attempted to study the physiology and psychology of yogis, fakirs and primitive trance states. We know that certain individuals can exercise conscious control over their breathing rates, their bodily temperature and heart frequencies. Buddhist monks have sat for forty-eight hours, apparently unharmed in the icy cold of the Himalayan snows. In the last few years, the science of bio-feedback has achieved some temporary success in teaching people to minimally lower their pathological blood pressures.

But it is only when one witnesses these extreme human behaviours personally and when one is confronted by the overwhelming evidence of one's personal senses, that the boundaries of reality and human potential suddenly become less certain, less predictable and some of our scientific explanations for human behaviours suddenly appear naive and simplistic.

There are more things in heaven and earth ...
(Hamlet, Act I, line 165)

It Does Not Belong To Us

It was cold, wet, windy and miserable as we left the northern suburbs of the city of Perth in the middle of the Australian winter. Our elderly Kombi felt tiny and vulnerable as we commenced the northward journey to Darwin. Two spare wheels, extra petrol, portable fridge, a large supply of tinned food and packets of dehydrated soups were all crammed neatly into the small yet ingeniously designed cupboard spaces. Spare gas cylinders, heavy duty car jacks, lamps and spare clothes were all included as we departed somewhat apprehensively to drive through some of the world's most isolated country towards the tropical "Top End".

Our apprehension was somewhat misplaced as before long we discovered there were many more intrepid travellers pursuing the thin ribbon of road around Australia. True, the distances are great and the sense of isolation can be quite profound. At times the road becomes so unsurfaced, rutted and dusty that we thought the Kombi would be shaken apart. However, there are oases of civilization euphemistically referred to as "roadhouses" every 300 or 400 kilometres. Here, both vehicle and occupants can refill with appropriate fuel for the next stage. At these isolated hostelries, we met fellow travellers, many who, having come from the opposite direction, passed on useful information concerning road and weather conditions ahead.

At the end of the day, one can usually arrange to arrive at a well equipped campsite. Here, the Kombi roof was elevated, the gas stove lit and in the small "home away from home", the essentials of domestic life continued.

In the well equipped communal washrooms, there was always informed discussion about the intrigues that lay ahead, the quality of future campsites and the scenic views not to be missed.

As the flat, monotonous wheat belt plains receded behind us, the russet and green grandeur of the Pilbarra and Kimberley geology and the upland ranges opened before us like a geological kaleidoscope. Gorges, ravines, waterfalls and exotic birds were everywhere, and as European suburbanites, we felt humbled, tiny and awed.

With increasing distance from the landmarks of civilization, our small car radio gradually faded to a few faint crackles and finally became silent wherever we turned the dial. As the familiar chatter of our culture vanished, the increasing presence of Aboriginal people was unavoidable. The small arid, isolated towns which cling to the edge of the desert was where we began to meet these real Australians. They sit in groups in the local dusty park, talking animatedly together, sometimes in loud voices, always in a language utterly different in form to any we had heard previously. Excited children chased each other, seemingly oblivious to purulent discharges from their ears, noses or eyes. We saw others sitting or standing by the roadside, dressed in old dirty clothes, motionless and staring into infinity. On the edge of towns, there were more little groups of shabbily dressed people sitting in dried up creeks, usually surrounded by piles of empty aluminium cans, rubbish and emaciated-looking dogs.

The further north we drove, the more difficult it became to avoid awareness of this increasing misery and maladaption. In the vast open spaces of the Kimberley, we saw huge herds of cattle which roamed the enormous ranches (and sometimes strayed onto our road) which earn fortunes for the already wealthy owners. It is these lands which for thousands of years was the territory of the families and tribes who now sit dejected and forlornly on the arid sterile verges of isolated towns. These poor people, the original owners, have been totally robbed of their ancestral lands which they possessed for thousands of generations. They were never consulted or remunerated. Worse still, their rights were never considered and they were simply replaced with cows.

For several years, they attempted to resist the invading Europeans, but inevitably the power of the gun overcame that of the spear, and around the turn of the century, they were rounded up and herded into reserves. Some were employed as stockmen in return for meagre subsistence benefits whilst others were placed into missions where many still live unto this day.

Until 1960, Aborigines were not acknowledged as citizens, counted as people or allowed to vote, and those who lived in towns were subjected to strictly enforced curfews. This unjust, illegal and immoral action which is now part of Australian history can never be reversed. There is a new Commonwealth Lands Title Act giving Aboriginal people the right to claim back what they can legitimately prove were their ancestral territories. But there are still many in high places who oppose even this gesture.

The health of indigenous Australian people when compared to the rest of the nation is poor, many of the statistics resembling those of developing countries rather than a western one, despite millions of dollars and much human effort being poured into far ranging health services and programmes.

A recent study carried out by the Australian Institute of Health and Welfare has highlighted some of these inequalities. All the indices for mortality rates, life expectancy, infant mortality, alcoholism, diabetes, cardiovascular disease and imprisonment are all much higher amongst Aboriginal people.

At birth, an Aboriginal boy's life expectancy is 18 years less than of his non-Aboriginal counterpart. 30% maternal deaths in Australia are in Aboriginal mothers, yet they only represent 3% of all confinements. In the Northern Territories, 73% of infant deaths are Aboriginal, yet only 38% of births are registered as Aboriginal. These and many more are sad statistics indeed.

Aboriginal people by nature tend to be quiet, unassertive and unconcerned with such western concepts as future, corporate profit and business investment, and are more concerned about the land, spirituality, relationships and family ties. One hot evening as we drove into the dusty tatty township of Halls Creek we were awed by the majestic backdrop of ancient arid mountains glowing crimson in penetrating light of the late afternoon tropical sunset. On the edge of town two friendly Aboriginal men were loading firewood onto the back of a Toyota truck, returned our waves and smiles. As they receded into a small speck in our driving mirror, we experienced a sensation of sadness and despair aware that this magnificent ancient and remote land had been stolen from somebody else and that somehow we should try and return as much of it as possible to the rightful owners.

Carl Jung wrote that modern man lives in material abundance but in spiritual poverty. Surely, without territory, there can be no sense of connectedness or spirituality. Without spirituality, health is severely compromised. Let us hope it is not too late for some of these injustices to be reversed.

At the white mans school, what are we taught?
Are they told the battles of our people?
Are they told of how our people died?
Are they told why our people cried?
Australia's true history is never read.
But the black man keeps it in his head.

Anonymous aboriginal poem

SOUP THERAPY

A young Aboriginal boy, approximately 17 years of age, was sitting on a jagged piece of rust-coloured rock. In his hand, he grasped an old bent fork and was energetically attacking a lamb chop half submerged in a bowl of soup. A large lump of bread and a half empty bottle of Johnny Walker sat on the dusty ground beside him. He wore a pair of dirty, torn, grey flannel trousers and a filthy, yet expensive, white shirt. It was his black leather shoes which singled him out, as his colleagues were either barefoot, wearing old rubber thongs or faded sneakers.

This sad scene occurred on the outskirts of Kalgoorlie, a flat, dusty, straggling city on the edge of the arid Australian desert, which stretches away as far as the eye can see to the eastern horizon. It is the last centre of population on the Eyre highway stretching away into the distance like a thin ribbon for the next 1,000 miles to the eastern states beyond.

No one really knows the origins of the name and there are several opinions, but somehow the name rings true. Kalgoorlie exists for one single reason and that is because of the high deposit of gold concealed below the surface of the arid, red, dusty land. A popular and profitable weekend hobby is spending a day in the bush prospecting for small fragments of the precious metal with the aid of a hand-held metal detector. The climate is extreme. In the middle of summer, the hot dry winds often exceed 40°C, whilst on winter nights the thermometer may drop to -5°C. One of my aboriginal colleagues once described this latter disagreeable phenomenon as a "three dog night" reflecting a rather less than conventional method of keeping warm when sleeping under the stars.

Gold was the sole reason for Kalgoorlie's birth as in the middle of the 19th century, millions of people from the four corners of the earth joined in the great gold rush in the belief that they could fulfill their fantasies by making a fortune and thence return home to live in comfort and luxury for the rest of their lives. Sadly, most of them did not succeed. No one told them that the deposits of gold are far and few between and also extremely difficult to find. They were unprepared for the harsh heat or cold of the desert, the large distances, the lack of water, competition from others and diseases such as cholera, typhus and TB. The enormous cemetery on the outskirts of the town is a silent, macabre testimony to the hardships and suffering that occurred, and a fascinating lesson in history for those who like to view ourselves in the context of what has gone on before.

Kalgoorlie boasts some of the widest streets in the world reflecting the original transportation system which were camel trains which requiring a large turning circle. Also obvious are splendid buildings and unique architecture built in the expectation of a permanently booming city, a dream that sadly was never realised. The hills around the town are artificial having been created over the last century by the constant tipping of excavated soil rock and debris extracted from hundreds of miles of tunnels and holes in the eternal quest for the precious metal. The largest man-made hole in the world just north of the town and one can only gasp in awe, standing on the crater edge, peering down over 500 metres to the bottom or the 4 kilometres across the crater. As long as gold continues to be found, it will continue to grow and it is estimated that eventually the chasm will exceed 5 kilometres in diameter.

Not surprisingly, Kalgoorlie is a masculine town. This is not to say that there are no women. It is just that the majority of the elements contributing to the overall ethos carry the stamp of a very large Y chromosome. The hotels and drinking houses are unsophisticated, rough and reminiscent of Western movie style frontier towns. Inside them, the noise is loud, basic and masculine. Drinking occurs in an ambience of unrefined crudity. Tattoos, sleeveless shirts, axillary hair in abundance, large dirty boots, unwashed hands, beer bellies, unshaven faces and solar keratotic skins dominate the bars. Drinkers are frequently served by large, nubile, late-adolescent girls called "skimpies", a term referring to the thin tight nylon blouses which cover but do not conceal more than adequate bouncing mammary glands upon which male customers goggle lustfully and without embarrassment.

The final stamp of archaic maleness is an entire street near the centre of town which is a 100-metre stretch of shop window brothels in which women of all shapes, sizes and races entice the isolated male voyeurs (known as pervs in Australia) to enter (for an agreed price) and act out their carnal fantasies.

This brief pastiche is the Kalgoorlie the visitor sees: the brashness, the vulgarity, the history, the architecture and of course the winners and their wealth. Carl Jung once remarked that every human action brings about both good and bad. So, who and where are the losers in Kalgoorlie and how do they suffer. In order to find out, I joined one of my younger colleagues on the "Kalgoorlie Soup Run". He was an enterprising ex-psychiatric nurse and he picked me up in the late afternoon at the small airport and drove me through the suburbs and wide tree-lined streets of this bustling if slightly brash frontier town, past the impressive Town Hall, and the bronze statue of Paddy Hannan, finally delivering me to the delightful Goldfields Hotel in the centre of town. My upstairs room was large and spacious, and opening up onto a wide wooden balcony overlooking the main crossroads from where I could watch in silent anonymity. Despite its roughness, Kalgoorlie is a hospitable town, and after being entertained and introduced to some of the local night life, I retired early after learning I had to be up and ready by 5.00 a.m.

We arrived at the Soup Kitchen at about 5.10 a.m. It consisted of an old single storey wooden house surrounded by a balcony with a kitchen extension built on to the rear. Two large Aboriginal women were stirring four very large pans balanced on an old gas-stove. I peered into the boiling brew. It consisted of gallons of stock into which had been cast half potatoes, carrots and raw lamb chops, all of which bubbled and steamed vigorously, releasing a penetrating odour which might have been appetising at a later hour of the day. On arrival, we were greeted loudly and cheerfully, and I was introduced to a nurse from the Child Welfare Services, a couple of student nurses and a social worker from the local Aboriginal Medical Service.

After the final addition of two handfuls of salt and some black pepper, four large containers were carried carefully, one by one, by a large Aboriginal man who placed them in the rear of our Holden utility. The lids were tied down with old rope and tested to see if they were leak-proof. After some minor final adjustments, we set off on the bumpy road leading to the disused mining tips on the outskirts of Kalgoorlie.

Ten minutes later, we arrived at what first appeared to be an old car body dump on the edge of a dry paddock. Old oil drums, piles of bricks and plastic containers, old tyres: all lay, strewn about the dry dusty land. Initially, there was no one to be seen. Then, in the distance, I saw a smoking fire around what were apparently some old sacks. After a short toot on the horn, a mangy dog appeared, barked and skulked apprehensively towards us. Then the sacks seemed to move. They were not sacks at all, they were people and they shuffled slowly over to our Holden van. The air was still cold and their breath created whisps of condensation which hung about in the early morning air. Despite the apparent cheerful exchange of greetings, they looked far from happy. They wore old clothes, several layers thick, in order to ward off the penetrating chill. The men were unshaved and unwashed, the women had untidy, uncombed hair, and walked with a round-shouldered stooping gait. Many had poor rotten teeth, most had red eyes, and one still clutched half a flagon of cheap Mildura sherry. Soon, more people appeared. Many of them were children who had been sleeping in the old cars, huddling together for what bit of shared warmth they could manage. Most of the children had some infection of one sort or another, the commonest being purulent noses, ears and eyes.

They were obviously pleased to see us as they queued up for their large plates of steaming soup protein. Furthermore, they were willing to talk about their immediate problems and both Social Worker and Child Welfare Nurse were able to identify and discuss possible interventions and alternatives for them and their children. This was much more than just an altruistic mobile feeding station. This was a community health team which had broken down the dilemmas of distrust and was able to establish links with the sad, forgotten people who were the original residents of Kalgoorlie and the surrounding gold fields area. Every day, the soup run continues to serve and ancillary workers are able to use this vital lifeline into the heart of this disinherited group of people. For the next two hours, we called at strategic points where similar groups of people living on the fringe of civilization greeted our arrival with pleasure and cordiality. I felt a sense of shame and humility, when one realizes that these decultured, friendly, dispossessed people are in this miserable predicament because the culture that dislodged them and acquired their land for its gold and minerals, are the same people who are now ironically feeding them with hot soup.

Perhaps the most distressing experience of the morning was at our final, stopping point. At the foot of one of the enormous slag heaps of dusty mine tailings, we met another group of approximately 25 people comprising 4 or 5 families. They clustered round the elevated tailgate of the ute, slurping their steaming soup, eating the large hunks of fresh dry bread noisily.

It was here that we met Andrew, the young man described at the beginning of our story. As he energetically consumed his breakfast, he informed me in a slightly slurred yet well educated voice that until recently, he had been attending one of Perth's private schools, having acquired an educational scholarship some years earlier. He was a successful student and a few weeks ago, achieved a high grade in his tertiary admission examination guaranteeing him a place at University. Rather than being delighted about his success, he experienced ambivalence, apprehension and confusion, as each step of the white man's ladder took him further from the culture to which somehow he really felt he belonged. From a culture which now only exists in the memories and minds of those who have descended from it. The culture that overtook them believed that gold and profit were of greater importance. Andrew's experience and dilemma eloquently describes and typifies the unhappy predicament of these sad, demoralised people. What should he do?

Later that morning, we all started work in a conventional manner either in offices, writing reports, visiting community centres, or seeing patients etc. But somehow, the really meaningful experiences of the day had all happened on the early morning soup run before we had started our formalised duties.

Sometimes, even today as I sit in my office, listening to some, depressed person lamenting about their perceived injustices, I am distracted by an intrusive image of these quietly spoken, dispossessed long-suffering people. They are the losers, still depending on the benevolence of others and on charities such as the early morning soup run to help sustain them in their otherwise joyless existence. As I sit, William Wordsworth's immortal lines which I learned more than 50 years ago intrude spontaneously into my consciousness:

> "If such is not nature's plan
> Have I not reason to lament
> What man has made of man."

(Lines written in the early spring by Wordsworth)

LUDWIG – A STORY OF STIGMA

Saturday mornings at the Hilton Hotel are always hectic. Today, the usual buzz of activity in the spacious and opulently furnished lobby was no exception. Overnight guests queued at the departure counter, porters pushed and fussed over large suitcases, delivery-men struggled with large boxes and top-hatted door attendants shouted taxis for apprehensive guests anxious to get to the airport on time.

On this Saturday morning, there was an extra commotion and a small group of excited people were clustered around the access doors and the lifts. They were talking and gesticulating animatedly, appearing oblivious to the comings and goings of the hotel guests as they struggled through the impatiently closing doors, dragging overloaded suitcases or reluctant children into the crowded lobby beyond. Further observation of this small group of people revealed that all this activity was focused on one young man whom the others were attempting to console and reason with. He was of slight build, with straight close-cropped hair, dark piercing eyes and a pale complexion. He wore light-coloured trousers, an open-necked striped shirt and a thin high buttoned jacket with a white handkerchief untidily stuffed into the top pocket. As his voice increased in volume and indignation, his strong German accent was clearly noticeable. Despite attempts by the deputy manager and his staff to pacify and reassure him, his voice could be heard by all, protesting loudly that they were wasting his extremely valuable time and if they insisted in detaining him any longer, the hotel would be held responsible and sued $1000 for every minute's delay.

As the situation escalated to an explosive pitch, the high-frequency whine of a police car siren was heard. Seconds later, with flashing blue lights, the squad vehicle pulled up in front of the hotel's revolving portal with its polished brass knobs and to the irritation of the top-hatted porter, three burly young policemen scrambled out and rushed across the red-carpeted hallway, pulling on their flat caps as they went. Their actions were so speedily executed that everyone, including the excited young man, were taken unawares and temporarily silenced.

However, within seconds, he had recovered his ire and was excitedly informing the fresh-faced young officers how he had been apprehended in his vitally important task of saving the world from inevitable destruction and irreversible catastrophe, a task which he believed he alone had been selected for and was planning to solve.

Not surprisingly, the guardians of the law were totally unconvinced of these utterances, and the young man was escorted physically to the waiting police vehicle, still protesting volubly, threatening damages of several millions for interfering and interrupting with a situation they were too dim-witted to comprehend. Ludwig (as he was called) was whisked off to the local police station where he was seen by the psychiatrist on call and committed to the nearest psychiatric hospital for further assessment in accordance with the regulations as laid down in the local mental health

This disturbing happening in one of the established city hotels was only one in a sequence of events in a process which had commenced several months previously. Ludwig was a young Austrian who, 3 years previously, gave up his hobby of mountain-climbing in his beloved Alps and sought adventure in Australia where he soon found work as an enterprising odd job and handyman. His reputation as a reliable tradesman soon grew and he acquired an old car, a small trailer and a rather dilapidated little house with a rear garden which soon filled with his tools, second hand household equipment, builders' sand and other essentials for his trade. Superficially, he was friendly with neighbours, but tended to isolate himself from local affairs, never establishing any relationship apart from acquaintances he would meet in the street or local delicatessen. It was noted that, when he was not working, he would spend much time watching television and seemed particularly concerned with issues relating to perceived injustices in the world as portrayed in documentaries and news programmes. On one of the rare occasions when he conversed, he expressed angrily to a man whose garden wall he was repairing that it was time that someone sorted out the world's problems once and for all.

It was soon after this outburst that Ludwig visited the conference manager of the Hilton and presented him with a neatly typed business card and booked the large conference suite for an international meeting of world leaders. Perhaps the manager did not quite understand what sort of world leaders Ludwig referred to or perhaps it was the aura of Teutonic efficiency or the sincerity of the crisp Austrian accent and the well-pressed jacket and dark tie that convinced him of the seriousness of the request, and the booking was duly made entitled "World Leaders' Forum", and Ludwig was given an official receipt for the $100 deposit and a collection of brochures, menus and attractions in and around the hotel to suit the interest and spectrum of tastes of all potential guests.

Months later, when the full story unfolded, it was discovered that Ludwig had drawn up a list of over 30 countries which he regarded as vital, powerful and important to the balance of future stability of the world and its peoples. From this carefully typed-out list, he selected the names of national leaders and senior politicians and sent invitations to an important meeting at which they would construct a plan to ensure the future happiness, stability and peace of the world, each invitation being accompanied by a carefully typed letter, outlining the purpose of the gathering and the importance of their role as a participant. The tone of the attachment was factual, unemotional, to the point, but a little vague as to what the procedures of the meeting would be. The whole symposium was to be chaired by Ludwig himself as he had the advantage of being a non-politician, therefore unbiased by any form of vested interest. The letters were signed under his own name with the simple title "Chairman – World Federation for Peace".

As the months passed, Ludwig went about his business in his usual industrious and efficient way. His reputation, reliability and high standards of workmanship ensured him a constant supply of work which busy home-owners either had not the time or lacked the technical skills to do themselves. Despite his eccentricity and reclusiveness, he was accepted by the neighbours because he was quiet and "never caused any trouble".

Not surprisingly, no-one knew of his plan to meet with world leaders or his personal involvement to clear the world of human greed, intolerance, war and injustice. Nor did the neighbours know that out of the 30 invitations, there were only 4 responses in the two months that followed: one was a polite response from 10 Downing Street, thanking him for his kind invitation but informing him that the Prime Minister already had an important meeting in Brussels the same weekend. A brief note came from the White House thanking him for his consideration of global issues. A two-page document in indecipherable script came from Tokyo, and a rather offhand dismissive letter from the Foreign Affairs Department in Malaysia informed him they had already arranged a much larger and more comprehensive meeting in Kuala Lumpur later in the year, which really made Ludwig's symposium redundant.

Most people would have despaired at such a poor response to their personal plans. Not so Ludwig. He reasoned that 26 non-responses should be interpreted positively as an indication of acceptance, and he proceeded to phone local caterers to arrange food and refreshments for the day. He also contacted a couple of local T.V stations, informing them of the important event when the world federation for peace was to meet in a few weeks' time in the city. He was surprised at their apparent lack of interest, but they did promise they might send a team down on the day if they had some spare people, but he should remember it was the same weekend as the one-day cricket match against the West Indies.

Convinced of the success of his venture and of the important role he was playing, he somehow "just knew" that on the day in question, the important participants would all turn up and he would play a leading role in changing the direction of civilisation for the better, after centuries of international squabbling, fighting, oppression, injustice and prejudice. After this week-end, it would all be different and he, Ludwig, would have been the principal orchestrator who, alone, had had the courage, conviction and drive to put a stop to the old evil ways and replaced them with a new set of values, goals and direction enabling mankind to live in peace and harmony for evermore. "Wonderful".

As described earlier, Ludwig was taken to a "place of safety" by the local constables, this being the euphemistic term for the police lock-up where people are detained for any number of reasons whilst a further decision is made about their future disposal. In Ludwig's case, this was until he had been assessed by the Duty Psychiatrist on call for that day. Unfortunately there was a 2-hour delay between the Police Sergeant's phone call to the hospital and the arrival of the doctor, a delay which inflamed the situation considerably and Ludwig (unaware that no international dignitaries had in fact turned up at the Hilton) began threatening the metropolitan force with damages of several thousands for every wasted minute of his time. Predictably, this only served to confirm the policemen's conclusions that he fitted firmly into their view that he was a "fruitcake". Being 10.30 a.m on a Saturday morning, it was time for morning tea and because no more calls had been received at the station, they could watch the opening television coverage of the one-day match against the West Indies.

Being a resourceful individual, Ludwig soon realised that his verbal protestations were in vain and he embarked on another strategy. In a corner of the tiny cell was a small stone bench, a steel seat-less toilet and a cold water tap and hand-basin. Removing his socks (the police already having taken his belt and shoes), he stuffed one into the small plug-hole. Yesterday's newspaper kindly left by the previous occupant was rolled into large balls and rammed into the depths of the toilet, effectively blocking the U-band escape route. He flushed the toilet which quickly filled up to the brim. Whilst waiting for the cistern to refill, he turned on the tap full force which soon filled the sink, which thence cascaded onto the floor below. This small stream was soon augmented to a substantial deluge as the toilet cistern once again refilled, was flushed. A pulsating flow of water gushed through the cell door, quickly covering the few metres to the police staff-room where within a few minutes, it had formed a mini-dam several centimetres deep.

So engrossed in the cricket were the police officers that it was several minutes before the increasing trickle seeping under the door was noticed. Then, pandemonium! Leaping to his feet, the nearest officer made the fatal mistake of opening the door. As the heavy wood door swung inwards before the accumulating pressure, a wave of scummy water sloshed into the policemen's sanctuary. There were curses and shouts drowning out the droning cricket commentary which a few seconds earlier had been the sole focus of their attention. Nor was this the end of their plight for the key-hole had been stuffed solid with lumps of soggy newspaper. Ludwig sat passively, yet triumphant on the stone-bench, his bare feet elevated and dry, and as the distraught officers fought with the jammed lock, innocently pressed the flush, releasing yet another torrent of bubbling frothy water.

Most mental health acts devote several pages to procedures and criteria for compulsory admission to an approved psychiatric hospital. While there is a wide variation amongst these acts, there are 2 basic criteria which must be fulfilled before anyone can be admitted involuntarily. First it must be established that the person is indeed suffering from a recognised and agreed mental illness, and secondly the person's behaviour is of such a nature and degree that s/he is a danger to himself or to others (or both).

It is clear that both these criteria can never be established with absolute certainly as the person may be feigning illness and the establishment of dangerousness is at best a prediction of the future and can only ever be an opinion albeit by an expert.

When the chaos and mess in the police station was finally sorted out, Ludwig was seen by a psychiatrist and committed for 28 days' assessment and treatment. We will never know what evidence the doctor had that Ludwig had a categorised mental illness or why in his opinion he believed he was potentially dangerous or whether commitment was simply the easiest and most convenient solution to a very unusual and inconvenient situation on a Saturday morning. No-one involved in this bizarre sequence of events would deny Ludwig's child-like illogicality of reasoning the impaired judgement and the almost paranoid grandiosity in the execution of his plan. There is no denying his absolute conviction that he alone could alter the direction of the world's future, nor could his intentions be seen in any other way than naively altruistic.

Naive, childish perhaps, irrational, but dangerous to others or himself? Much more difficult to establish. Ludwig certainly did not believe he was mentally ill, but he was treated in hospital much against his will with anti-psychotic medications which made him drowsy, gave him a dry mouth, caused him to be constipated and to develop a fine tremor in his limbs. His vision, whilst also blurred, caused him considerable difficulty in reading. Furthermore, none of the treatments changed his views and he remained indignant that a golden opportunity for world peace had been missed by the bungles of the local police and mental health services.

While in hospital, he developed a confiding relationship with a couple of nurses and his medical registrar to whom he described other grandiose schemes and ideas. One in particular stands out. He had already commenced planning a one-man expedition to scale Mount Everest (remember he was an experienced alpinist). Once at the summit, he would take a photograph of himself, which he would then sell for $5 each, thus ensuring a large fortune. Curiously, he confided this information to the middle-aged, overweight cigarette-smoking registrar who he correctly assumed would never even contemplate this project, whereas the slimmer and fitter consultant in charge might just think it a brilliant idea and beat him to the summit. Predictably, Ludwig was assessed, given a psychiatric diagnosis and contrary to his wishes, commenced on standard medications for the illness in question. These certainly tranquillised him, he became less energetic and soon lost the strength of his many odd and eccentric ideas. At the end of 28 days, his compulsory status terminated and he declined to remain in hospital voluntarily as he did not believe he had an illness and his work appointments were already a month behind. Fortunately, he had acquired a friendly relationship with many of the staff and agreed to attend the Outpatient Clinic periodically. He was less enthusiastic about continuing with the stupefying medications.

There are many like Ludwig whose bizarre and eccentric ideas are probably the external manifestation of underlying mental illness but there are others whose odd ideas are probably not due to definitive underlying disorder. Hunderds of people were compulsorily admitted to psychiatric hospitals in the old U.S.S.R during the mid-seventies and eighties and forcibly treated were said to be "ill" because they held political views contrary to the prevailing communist regime and were therefore said to be delusional and unreal.

The application of the insanity label is thus an easy way of removing someone who is a public nuisance and whose views are a threat to the stability of the prevailing socio-political system. This is of course a purposeful misinterpretation of the concept of dangerousness as implied in all mental health acts.

It is doubtful whether Ludwig was ever dangerous either to himself or to others, and hence whether his initial compulsory admission was legal. Regrettably, the insanity label tends to become a permanent stigma and once labelled, the person's future behaviour and non-conformitism is forever regarded with suspicion of mental illness, thus facilitating further episodes of compulsory hospital treatment. Sadly, Ludwig's second admission was an example of this "Here he is again" phenomenon.

It was shortly after midnight when a white police car pulled up by the river on a chilly and clear winter's evening. So far, all had been quiet and the two officers had a few more hours of the late shift to complete. They removed their flat caps, released their seat-belts, and sat back for a relaxing smoke before moving off to the next part of the evening's circuit. Before the first match was struck, a second car pulled up behind them. This was an older and noisier vehicle and as the driver applied the hand-brake, it was obvious that it could benefit from an oil can. The driver turned off the headlights, but the sidelights were sufficient to illuminate clearly the outline of the 2 reclining constables. Then, there was silence and no movement. The police driver squinted in the rear-view mirror where he could see the outline of a thinnish person sitting eerily and still, as if simply watching.

Irritated and cross, the officers quickly re-adjusted their uniforms, extinguished their cigarettes, started the engine and slowly cruised away through the wealthy riverside suburbs to a small, isolated car-park adjacent to a concrete boat ramp where they hoped to recommence their nocturnal siesta. Unfortunately, the peace they sought was denied them as once more the mystery vehicle pulled up besides them, and they could now see his shadowy silhouette as he gazed impassively in their direction. The young police driver could stand it nor more. He leapt out of the car and scurried around to speak to the sinister intruder. "What the hell are you doing, mate?" asked the irritated constable. The driver gently pushed the glaring torch out of his eyes and in a quiet steady voice, responded '1 am checking up on your movements, constable, in order to confirm that you are fulfilling your professional duty and not wasting public time and expense."

This was not the usual exchange the policeman was accustomed to at 1.00 a.m. Furthermore, he was not pleased about someone else checking on his movements. "Who the hell are you?" the irate custodian of the law demanded. "I am a concerned rate-payer and citizen expressing my rights," the young man replied. "What is more, I have taken a note of your number and I am going to report you for being discourteous to a member of the public."

The policeman felt the blood rising in the back of his head and the hair bristling around his sweaty collar. Deciding the best response was no response, stormed back to his car, climbed in, slammed the door, reversed out and accelerated away in a fury. As the car sped along the freeway, a sense of familiarity and recognition slowly dawned. He remembered that crisp, clear, German accent as belonging to the "nutter" who had flooded the police station several months ago and proceeded to tell his colleague of the inundation story.

The speeding police car slowed down and pulled over into a deserted side lane on the main bridge into town, and the driver described in detail to his colleague the pandemonium of that Saturday morning and of the mess that had taken days to clear up. As he spoke, he was still aware of the stinging reprimand that they had all received for failing to exercise due vigilance and care for someone in the lock-up. Even recounting these earlier events evoked a sense of fury in the young constable, a feeling which was heightened as predictably a few minutes later, Ludwig's old car glided ghost-like to a squeaky standstill behind them.

This time, there was no hesitation or mystery. Ludwig was briskly pulled out of his vehicle, handcuffed and manhandled into the rear of the police car, and driven without courtesy to the local psychiatric hospital a couple of miles away. By now, it was 5.30 a.m and a grey dawn was breaking as the policemen rang the bell on the acute admission ward. The door was duly opened by a weary-looking nurse who recognised Ludwig from the previous admission a few months earlier. Despite protests about freedom and human rights, Ludwig was pushed into the fetid gloom of the admission ward corridor. The nurse was given a brief outline of the circumstances leading to this action, and then before any further discussion, the harassed officers dashed to the car, engine still ticking over, and sped off as the lock on the heavy admission ward door clunked too.

This unilateral action by the police was of course illegal and unjustified. Ludwig was not on any form of community treatment order, he was an ordinary free citizen. His actions in pestering the police were not illegal and although eccentric and bizarre, were not a threat or a danger to himself or to anyone else.

Ludwig, like many others, is a victim of modern stigma and prejudice. As long as he lives, this malignant social disability will remain like the Ancient Mariner's albatross around his neck. His future attempts to be accepted as an ordinary member of the community will be compromised, denying his rights as a citizen. Once the stamp of mental illness has been applied, it adheres like a sticky label triggering a self-reinforcing cycle of negative public imagery, perpetuating the ostracism, exclusion and alienation, phenomena which themselves then become the external stressors which in turn create more stress and anguish to the unfortunate person who through no fault of his own has at some time suffered the appellation "mentally ill". There are many who, not so stigmatised, have odd and omnipotent ideas and whose reality boundaries differ from the majority, but without this diversity of opinion, the world of art, music and literature would become stultified, boring and barren.

As modern civilisation lurches irrationally towards global uniformity, yielding to the persuasive forces of an insatiable commercial media and the powerful norms of fashion, intolerance to even mild forms of public deviance and eccentricity diminishes. Those who suffer from what are presently called "mental health problems" will continue to be marginalised and remain the victims of stigma. It is little more than a century ago that the mentally ill were labelled "imbeciles, lunatics and insane" and were the objects of ridicule, mirth or fear. The regressive tendency to return to these more primitive responses must be energetically and rationally disputed and defended against.

THE MANY FACES OF ALCOHOLISM

Alcoholism – A compulsion to drink that causes harm.

Whilst this definition may appear some what simplistic it conceals a complex spectrum of human problems which may present in a variety of ways,often when unexpected and in people who it was never suspected had a problem.

The two following vignettes are examples of unusual presentations which caught everyone by surprise.

MIKE

Reputations of pubs usually reflect the nature and temperament of the landlord and his assistants. The establishment may be 300 years old with the original oak beams spanning low ceilings and there is probably an open log fire crackling under an ancient stone mantle shelf to welcome the weary and dampened walker. True, the quality of the beer is important but, if there is a surly landlord, lacking in empathy or welcoming skills, the place will never be successful and the public, perceptive to these social vibrations, will inevitably be aware and vote with their feet!

The Fox Inn is not one of these "blacklisted" places. On the contrary, it has a reputation for conviviality, a relaxed atmosphere, good beer, above-average food and, a homely ambience. This is not surprising, as the pub is a converted cottage and the adjoining wall between two rooms has been demolished into one drinking area. The bar is somehow the remains of where the kitchen used to be, whilst a spare room at the rear houses a long wooden table where people may sit twelve aside (fourteen at a squeeze) for the frequent small birthday celebration or wedding reception. Additionally, there is frequently discussion and debate as Mike (the landlord), his family and clients struggle with clues to the Guardian or Independent crossword. To assist in these intellectual activities, the shelf above the bar houses the Oxford Standard Dictionary, a Thesaurus and several other literary books including a Penguin entitle quite simply "Usage".

This congenial ambience and activity reflects and is generated by the management style of the landlord. He is short, muscular and like many who are prematurely bald, covers the top of his head with long hair swept forwards from the sides and back. He is moderately overweight, most of the excess being on his abdomen, which tends to protrude amply above his low slung trouser belt line. Originally, he came from the next village where he went to school and acquired the nickname of "podge", a term referring to his stature. Early in his academic career, he showed musical talent, learned to play the banjo, and to this day, still performs with the nearby town band at Christmas and other annual festivities. After leaving school, he went to University and acquired a degree in Mechanical Engineering, and for several years, whilst his children were young, worked for an international engineering company. In his mid-forties, he grew restless and sought new direction, and so decided to return to his origins, and by good fortune bought the Fox Inn, which had just become available following the death of the previous landlord.

Knowing the local culture and being sensitive to the attitudes and views of the locals, the establishment soon became popular with a large clientele, mostly local, but many from several miles away. With his knowledge of local affairs and his intellectual skills and University training, he could, like most good publicans, enter into dialogue and discussion on any topic under the sun. Concurrently, he would usually be sipping a glass of the local excellent best bitter and smoking a cigarette in a posture of earnest wisdom. His success was essentially due to his quiet and genuine interpersonal style, for he was not in any way extroverted or insincere, and could be described as phlegmatic and sober.

One Saturday morning, Mike complained to his wife (a part-time physiotherapist) that he was not feeling well. He was experiencing vague abdominal pain, and a sensation of nausea and bloatedness in the pit of his stomach. He had also noted that his stools had been unusually black and tarry, but rationalised this as being due to the Guinness he had drunk the previous evening. Such was his malaise that he could only manage a piece of lightly buttered toast for breakfast. Ten minutes later, he clutched his abdomen to soothe the increasing stabbing sensations. His wife noticed that he looked pale and ashen, and small beads of perspiration clung to his forehead. As he rose from the table, he experienced a rising wave of pressure in the back of his throat followed by a sudden, overwhelming nausea. He staggered and rushed to the downstairs toilet where he commenced to eject copious amounts of bright red vomit, which was quite obviously not Guinness. Mike did not remember the ambulance journey to the hospital. He could not recall the high speed ride with the bell ringing and lights flashing. Nor did he have any memory of being transferred and taken to the Operating Theatre, where the surgeon passed an endoscope down his oesophagus in order to tie off the enlarged gushing blood vessels which had almost caused his demise.

It was only when he awoke in the Intensive Care Department and saw the collection of life supporting tubes, wires, pumps and screens that he realised, something very, very serious had happened to him.

For many years Mike had shared with his customers the delights and pleasures of discussing and debating politics, science, religion and how to correct and rebalance the instability of the world, and the irrational behaviour of homo sapiens who inhabited most of its surface. He had patiently listened to sad stories of failed marriages, businesses and sporting events, and had acquired many counselling skills to help the bereaved and those with other losses. With the help of his Thesaurus and dictionaries, he and his clients had successfully completed many hundreds of crossword puzzles.

Accompanying all these endeavours, he had continuously yet slowly consumed the golden liquid from his cellar below. For years, this had trickled down into his ever-expanding stomach, where it was absorbed into his circulating blood system. Some would pass through his duodenum and small intestine where more would enter the circulating system of veins and transport it speedily to every corner of his body. The effect on his brain was the pleasant euphoria and sense of well-being, whilst the kidney's response was to increase urine output in order to eliminate what it regarded as a foreign substance.

The most important organ was Mike's liver to which the alcohol-laden blood passes before returning to the general circulation. For years, his liver cells had struggled to cope with the constant bombardment of alcohol molecules, and the complex biological detoxification systems had converted the alcohol into its harmless molecular constituents, before eliminating it into the safety of the bile. Unfortunately for Mike, the necessary enzyme systems responsible for this process had become overloaded and begun to fail like an overworked bilge pump in a leaking boat. The pressure in his liver had increased to such an extent that it had dammed back to the floppy blood vessels in his upper intestine and stomach, and they had become distended, enlarged, fragile and like big bright, thinly-skinned, pulsating cherries.

Finally, on the Saturday morning in question, the pressure was so great that the delicate vessels simply burst open, perhaps punctured by a sharp corner of toast, thus releasing the torrent of blood into the cavity of his stomach and adjoining intestines.

We know the rest of the story. Due to prompt action, a speedy ambulance service and a rapid blood transfusion, Mike is still alive today, but has to exercise great caution as only a third of his original liver cells remain, the rest having been irreversibly damaged by years of slow alcohol poisoning. Perhaps in the future, liver transplants will become as common as hip replacements. In the meantime however, thousands of apparently normal people are going to bleed to death because they are totally unaware that their livers can no longer cope with the daily excessive load of alcohol in whatever form the drinker enjoys. Mike continues to entertain and debate with his clientele and will probably continue to do so as long as he insists on accompanying these activities by drinking iced water or soda and lime, but somehow it is not quite the same!

ELSIE'S CATS AND RATS

Elsie lived alone in a neat little house on the corner of the street. There was a small front garden, comprising a manicured lawn bisected by a white gravel path, leading up to a brightly coloured front door opening inwards from a small porch and a white step where she would carefully place the empty milk bottle each evening and retrieve the full fresh one left by the early morning delivery man.

On either side were neatly trimmed privet hedges in front of which were carefully chosen flowers, bedded according to the appropriate season. Elsie was well known in the neighbourhood. She was usually in the garden, and frequently could be seen conversing over the small white wooden gate at the end of the path. Sometimes she was to be found in the corner store, where she would spend time talking to friends purchasing her Bristol Cream sherry and other goods. For years she had been a regular church attender, and on the fourth Saturday of each month was on the roster ensuring that altar flowers and the general state of the church were ready for the Sunday services. She had followed this existence since her husband died five years ago (on her birthday) from a sudden heart attack, and apart from a few legal problems with the will, she appeared to have coped. She had gathered together his clothes, compact discs, record collection and other personal memorabilia and locked them away in a small box room off the hall, and then continued with life as if nothing untoward had happened.

It is not true to say that she lived alone, as since her husband's death she had acquired three cats. All of them were strays, but one by one they had been seduced by her care and concern and fresh, tempting pieces of fish and meat upon which they had grown plump and complacent. Each had its own small wicker basket with its individual woolly blanket, which was carefully washed each week. Whether Elsie was sitting watching TV, working in the garden or talking over the garden gate, one could be sure that the cats would either be sitting comfortably nearby, aimlessly loitering in the flowerbeds, or nuzzling her ankles with their furry faces.

Today was very different. Elsie was in the local hospital, recovering from a small operation to remove cataracts which had for some time been the cause of her deteriorating eyesight. Before coming into hospital she had made elaborate arrangements with Mrs Green (her neighbour), not only to feed the cats but to check on their welfare morning and evening. She instructed the milkman to cancel the daily pint of semi-skimmed and asked the postman not to leave any parcels on the doorstep. She turned on the small brass table lamp in the hall, believing this would deter any potential robber.

The operation was surprisingly quick and painless. She had almost enjoyed it. Just a few drops of an anaesthetic in the eye, lots of bright lights and the blurred outline of green coated, friendly doctors and nurses leaning over her, chatting as they painlessly snipped away her opaque lenses. The whole procedure was completed in less than an hour, and she was assured that, after an overnight stay, she could return home the next morning. Unfortunately, because of the bandage over her eyes, she was unable to take advantage of the ward television and the evening programme, but there seemed to be plenty of friendly people on the ward to talk to. It was quite different to what she imagined hospital would be like.

About nine o'clock Elsie felt a little strange. She experienced a funny mixture of tiredness, yet simultaneously was restless. She felt anxious, even slightly fearful, that something odd and unexplained was going on which she was unable to put into words. She rang the buzzer and told the young nurse that she would like to go to sleep, as she thought that the stress and excitement of the last two days was "catching up". The nurse agreed, and turned off the main light, leaving only the dim wall lamp glowing above the bed.

As she tried to sleep in this strange new bed, background noises of the ward seemed to increase in intensity. The faint voices of unknown others seemed to be particularly clear. She wondered if they were nurses or perhaps other patients who were still awake, or possibly watching the television. She turned onto her side, pulling the sheet over her ear, hoping it would give her the peace she required for somnolence. Paradoxically, the opposite occurred. The distant voices were somehow coming nearer and clearer. She thought she heard her name mentioned. This really startled her and she began to feel concerned. "Why should they be talking about me?" she mused to herself. Before she was able to respond to her own question, she overheard the word "get" uttered by one of the distant speakers. This was followed by a burst of laughter. By now she was very alarmed and commenced reassuring herself that she was imagining it all, or simply misinterpreting the innocent conversations of nurses in the office. Such was her anxiety however, that she experienced the bristling of her hair and tingling on the back of her neck. The sensations moved down her spine and created a fearful shiver. A few seconds later, she became aware of the pressure of the bedclothes on her toes and ankles, causing her to recoil her feet. She was now very frightened and felt herself sweating. Her mouth was dry and she began to panic. She tried to lie still, but it was no good. The sensation at the base of the bed increased and changed into an intense itching, almost as if something was gnawing the skin around her ankles. At this point another shrill, almost menacing burst of laughter came from somewhere along the corridor, reinforcing her sensations of fear and panic.

Suddenly, there was a sharp needle-like pain in her left ankle. It was as if someone had stuck a pin into the delicate skin in her Achilles' tendon. In desperation she pulled off the sheets and sat up, terrified. She was aware of her own heart beating inside her chest. She tore the loose bandage off her eyes and looked around. Blurred images and shadows were all she could perceive, but a few seconds later she noticed a couple of vague shoe-like objects to the left of the dimly illuminated bedside locker. She tried to focus, but this only caused the shadows to flutter. Instantly she recognised them, not as shoes but as large rats. No wonder her legs were painful, and no wonder people were laughing. These terrible rodents had somehow climbed up the bed frame and had bitten her ankles as she tried to sleep. She looked again and noticed a huge flickering shadow on the wall, and then a loud creaking noise. Who could be doing these terrible things to her, and why? The flickering intensified and appeared to be creeping slowly towards the bed in a slimy, menacing manner. Terrified and bewildered, she shrieked out. and in desperation grabbed the small lamp on the bedside locker, and hurled it with all her might at the imaginary creatures on the nearby wall.

Seconds later, two astonished junior nurses rushed to her bed, switched on the light, and found her cowering and trembling on the floor, clutching the pillow close to her chest.

It was not until the young psychiatrist visited Elsie, that an explanation for her symptoms was made. She wrote in the case file: "This lady's perceptual disturbance and delusions of persecution are due to the delirium tremens. I recommended the appropriate treatment for alcohol withdrawal."

As noted previously, part of Elsie's routine included the daily intake of Bristol Cream sherry, which she regarded as being good for her circulation and for her sleep. She and her husband had drunk a glass or two before supper for many years, and it had become an established part of her daily routine, both at home and also when they went away on holiday. Following his death, Elsie found the sherry to be of great comfort, and had not only increased the amount (a glass in his memory!) but also had started to take one or two (occasionally three) before lunch. This gradual increase in daily consumption had occurred over several months, and she was always proud that she had never been even the "slightest bit under the weather". Nor had any of her friends been aware of her daily habit.

With the passage of time, Elsie' s body had become quite accustomed to this daily input of alcohol and had adjusted without any obvious ill effects. Her brain cells had adjusted so well that on several occasions she noted that, if for some reason she missed a couple of glasses, her concentration was not so good, and she felt a little tense or "twitchy" as she preferred to call it. Somehow, the constant presence of alcohol in her blood had now become a requirement, almost a necessity, as if she were dependent upon it for normal functioning. Not surprisingly physiologists refer to this state as dependence, or more specifically, biological or chemical dependence.

The cells in Elsie's brain had indeed become dependent, and actually required alcohol in order to function in a normal manner. Consequently, when the regular supply was cut off because of her hospitalisation, they became unco-ordinated and commenced to malfunction and misfire, resulting in the frightening perceptual experiences often referred to as hallucinations and delusions.

Delirium tremens (the D.T.s), or alcohol withdrawal syndrome, requires special treatment with the appropriate medical drugs before the underlying chemical imbalance is corrected.

There are many who for years have drunk alcohol every day for as long as they can remember. They have come to accept their habit as being as normal as taking a shower or brushing their teeth. Sometimes there has been a gradual increase over the years in the quantity consumed. Sometimes this has happened in association with a sad life event, such as a catastrophe or major loss. The unexplained grief and sadness associated with the death of her husband may well have been such an event, and for a time the sherry was of positive therapeutic value to Elsie. Without realising it, she had become dependent in a classical addictive manner.

Elsie's discharge and return to the comfort of her home and the reassuring company of her cats was thus delayed for nearly a week. Nowadays, following the advice of the friendly Alcohol Counsellor who still comes to visit her, she restricts herself to a single glass of sherry in the evening, about half an hour before her evening meal. She still has difficulty in actually believing that her experiences were due to too much sherry, and on a cold evening sitting at home with her cats, she is sometimes tempted to have another glass, but the frightening and vivid memory of the large rats that she was so convinced she saw and felt in the hospital quickly causes her to change her mind.

Mad, Bad or Sad

Eric Crossen blinked in the bright tropical sunshine. In front of him, the line of majestic king palm trees and casuarinas bordered Fox Hill Road and led northwards. A profusion of brilliant red poinciana trees dazzled his eyes, and the variety of colours from hundreds of bougainvillea, hibiscus, poinsettia and yellow Elder bushes caused him to catch his breath in awe.

It was not only the tropical beauty that overwhelmed his perceptions, but also the fact that only a minute earlier, the heavy studded wooden doors of Fox Hill Prison had briefly opened, allowing him to walk out after 18 months' confinement into the fresh free air beyond.

During his stay he had been an exemplary and compliant prisoner. The Superintendent himself had commented on his gentlemanly politeness and his courtesy. He had fulfilled his obligatory duties in the kitchen and the prison gardens without complaining, and had successfully engaged in a correspondence course in English literature with the College of the Bahamas. To maintain one's equanimity in old Colonial style, crowded prison is no mean feat. The wardens were not known for their tact, and his fellow inmates were an assorted mixture of Bahamians, Haitian refugees, Cuban rebels and an assortment of misfits from all over the Caribbean. He stood quietly for a few minutes, allowing the beauty of nature and the warm sunshine to absorb into his pale skin. After a couple of minutes of quiet contemplation, he realized that there was no alternative but to walk the 5 miles to Nassau town. Perhaps he might be fortunate enough in thumbing a lift once he reached Fox Hill Village at the end of the road. At this moment of decision, he noticed a large stationary left hand drive Buick parked by the side of the road. He hesitated, but before he could change direction, the doors opened and two smartly-dressed men in American tropical suits approached him.

One of them addressed him directly: "We would like you to help us with some enquiries." Eric sighed defeatedly and without further objection, climbed into the rear seat of the air-conditioned Buick which sped off in the direction of Nassau. Eric had a free lift to town, but a day later, his journey continued by aeroplane across the sea to Miami to help the F.B.I in their enquiries concerning the use of stolen cheques and forged credit cards three years earlier.

Eric Crossen first came to the attention of the local people when one morning he breezed into the Doctors' Common Room at the Princess Margaret Hospital and introduced himself to the dozen or so medical staff as they drank their mid-morning coffee, discussing the morning's activities. His entry was not a major event as the Doctors' Common Room was a cosmopolitan place and interesting medical people who were passing through would drop in, on the look-out for locum work or just to exchange ideas and anecdotes. Eric informed us that he was a Child Psychiatrist and although English, had been working for the past few years in Toronto, and was now taking a 6-month sabbatical leave in order to catch up on writing and research. At this time, there was no Child Psychiatrist in Nassau, and he seemed mildly surprised when someone suggested he might offer his services to the Health Department. He was quick to explain that he was not looking for paid work as his writing and research projects would take most of his spare time although he did offer to address one of our future continuing medical education meetings on a subject of his own interests.

Eric was very sociable. He was well-spoken and seemed to have a wide knowledge of many other subjects, sometimes

115

only indirectly related to medicine. We learnt that some years before entering psychiatry, he had been a cameraman for the National Geographical Society on an expedition to the mouth of the Amazon. His knowledge of the local Indian tribes seemed quite extensive, and he described how an American multinational razor blade company paid a large sum of money to conceal the secret of mudcakes that local native Indians applied to their faces to permanently remove the growth of facial hair.

Eric was about 35 years of age, always meticulously dressed in a white shirt, shorts, ankle-length socks and expensive cream and brown leather shoes. In his right hand, he usually carried an expensive-looking leather briefcase. His straight carefully cut hair was neatly parted on one side, his boyish face and general demeanour made him congenial and acceptable company, and within a couple of weeks, he was included and accepted in the circuit of most of the regular social events associated with the extensive expatriate medical circle. As time went by, it became apparent that Eric had crammed more experiences into his life than most of us. In addition to his national geographical experiences, we learnt that he had been an expedition Medical Officer in the Himalayas. He had some experiences in neurosurgery and spent some time in a famous European medical research centre.

His charm and affability did not pass unnoticed amongst some of the female members of the circle, especially some of the younger ones, and before long, a few discriminating eyebrows were raised when he was observed to be frequently in the presence of the daughter of one of the more affluent residents of Nassau. This concern was heightened by the knowledge that he had told someone else that back in Canada he had a wife and two children. Despite these peripheral blemishes, his general amiability and engaging manner were the salient and overriding traits. Another of his interests was tropical fish. Several very enjoyable afternoons were spent diving and trap scores of small brightly coloured purple gammas. These brilliant little reef fish inhabit the reefs 3 or 4 metres below the surface of the crystal-clear Bahamian waters. On one afternoon, we would catch scores of these little creatures using a special Perspex sucker gun poked into the nooks and crevices of the lower coral structure. On the surface, a small compressor fed air down a line attached to a scuba mouthpiece, thus permitting ambulation on the soft sandy bed of the ocean. Somehow, Eric had acquired this equipment from a local agent who also arranged for the afternoon's catch to be transferred into large water filled plastic bags, oxygenated and flown on the same day to Miami where we later learnt that they were sold "for a good price" to end up in exclusive aquariums.

After a few more weeks, some observers began to comment that for a man of 36 years of age, to have been involved in so many previous experiences was becoming difficult to believe. His credulity became more strained when late one evening, he described his experiences in an African leper colony, but seemed to have no real knowledge of the more recent types of drugs being used. A couple of days later (unknown to our circle of friends), we learnt that he had hired the local auditorium to show his film of life in an Amazonian village charging $5 entrance fee. Unfortunately, one of the audience recognized the film as being a National Geographical Society film made by a colleague some years previously, and not Eric Crossen.

Despite these gathering clouds of doubt over Eric's authenticity, no one seemed willing to either disbelieve or challenge some of his assertions. It was as if we all wished to believe that he was genuinely a rather charming and remarkable person.

Unfortunately, this conspiracy of dissociation only lasted for a few days as Eric was apprehended for trying to sell his young girl-friend's pearls which she had taken out of the family bank vault as a result of his persuasive charms. The following day he was arrested for signing stolen cheques in order to obtain funds to meet his extravagant and flamboyant lifestyle.

One remarkable aspect of Eric's fall from grace was his persistent insistence that he had not committed any crime and had always intended to pay back every cent as soon as his grandiose plans commenced making a commercial return. He explained that the money he had acquired was simply a rather unusual form of investment which very soon would bring profit, not just to him, but also to his friends who had so kindly made him these "loans". At no time did he ever admit to any evil intention. Such was his plausibility and skilled use of language that the senior investigating detective later admitted that after several hours' interrogation, he was almost persuaded by his plausibility and genuineness of his innocence.

Psychopaths are usually ordinarily-looking people physically, quite indistinguishable from others. They are to be found in every culture and have been recognized for hundreds of years in the history of all nations. They have been responsible for many of society's major problems, including financial catastrophes, political blunders, wars, crime and other human follies.

Paradoxically, they have also made major contributions to some of humankind's artistic creativity and achievements, sporting successes and acts of courage and bravery. Sadly, some of those who have been applauded and rewarded for their behaviours on the battle-field have subsequently been punished or sent to prison for their identical behaviour in ordinary civilian life.

It is a common misbelief that psychopaths are criminals, as the majority of people with psychopathic elements in their personality never break the law, and the media image of the cold, ruthless, con-man and murderer who kills people for trivial reward without remorse is fortunately a rare form.

Psychopathic people are usually characterized by their

tendency to anti-social behaviours and personality style. These traits include untruthfulness, insincerity, lack of guilt, remorse or shame, impulsiveness, pathological lying, and an inability to learn from experience or reason. Additionally, they are frequently charming, likeable, and demonstrate a plausibility enabling them to deceive others with ease. They have an intuitive ability to manipulate people and situations to their own advantage. Many, when confronted with their deceit, can display such indignation and feigned insult, that the accuser may experience guilt and shame. Nor surprisingly, an early description of psychopathy was "moral insanity".

There is no satisfactory explanation why some people become psychopathic, nor is there an accurate description of the condition as there are many different types. It is true that some are unable to keep out of trouble with the law, and it is estimated that 10-15% of the prison population are psychopathic. Students of personality, inform us that about 1% of the general population have obvious psychopathic characteristics and that a large proportion of these are unrecognized. Furthermore, the condition cannot be seen as an illness, and conceptually it is easier to view it as a sort of failure or incomplete development of the very essence of personality itself.

The most troublesome psychopaths are those who, having exceptional charm and the gift of higher intelligence, keep out of trouble and acquire high positions in business, in industry, the professions and the heights of politics. In these important areas of public life they can be quite devastating. They are able to manipulate their chosen system not for the altruistic goal of helping others, but solely for their own narcissistic and self centred wishes. This tendency to use others simply as objects for their own personal ends, is common to all psychopathic people.

Eric Crossen was a charming, engaging and sociable man. He was intelligent, creative, well-read and affable. He was also deceitful, emotionally detached and ruthless in his ceaseless attempts to manipulate other people and systems to his own self-centred goals. At no time, did he show any evidence of aggression, remorse, guilt or human worth. In some ways, he was the perfect example of a computerized robot, trained to interact socially and to use his intellect and thinking to work out the problems of survival. Unfortunately, like a computer, whilst his problem-solving skills were almost without fault, he had a complete absence of emotional reactivity without which human beings are unable to conceptualize right and wrong, good and bad, morality or immorality, concepts without which the tenuous structure of civilization would fall apart, thrusting us back into chaos. The majority of psychopathic people appear normal until we get to know them well. Usually, they do not appear depressed, anxious, perplexed or odd in their thinking, and it is probably incorrect to view them as suffering from some illness.

Whether psychopaths are seen as ill, insane or just bad, is probably irrelevant. What is important is that we remember they are always around, and it is at our peril if we fail to recognize their presence amongst us.

THE MOSS AND THE STONE

It was mid-August in Vancouver as I sauntered along the quay adjacent to the splendid, futuristic downtown Exhibition Centre. Beyond, lay the sparkling waters of the outer harbour and the majestic mountains of British Columbia as they reached up to the cotton wool clouds and the blue skies of an idyllic summer's day. Crafts of all sizes and forms criss-crossed the harbour and a clumsy-looking float-plane droned across the sky carrying visitors. The shadows were lengthening and there was a definite feeling of afternoon tea time as I sipped from a cup and saucer clearly marked "B.C. Exhibition Centre."

I was collecting my thoughts and reflecting on the last session on the biology of schizophrenia, when I was abruptly interrupted by a complete stranger. He addressed me without invitation, in an unmistakable Yorkshire accent:

"Are you attending this meeting?" he asked plaintively, eyeing my conference lapel badge.

"Yes," I replied, *"there must be nearly 2,000 of us altogether!"*

Without pausing for breath, he continued, *"So you must be a shrink?"*

This uninvited request for an appointment came from a rather short, stocky, dishevelled-looking, balding man in his mid 50s. He wore creased light coloured trousers, a crumpled checkered short-sleeved shirt and on his feet, were a pair of worn-out Reebok sport shoes. On his right arm was a faded tattoo of an anchor and he carried two or three days' unshaven facial hair. He seemed perplexed, unhappy, and had correctly assumed there was a probability that the first person he addressed would be a psychiatrist.

He pointed to a modern apartment block on the far side of the harbour. *"I've been here nearly twenty years,"* he impressed upon me. *"I've made a lot of money out of real estate, timber and property. I've had three children who've all grown up, become successful and left home. My wife left me three years ago and I now live by myself. Last month, I went on a trip to Hull to see my family. I've got three sisters, two brothers, some cousins and some old friends from my school days."*

At this point he sighed with despair, took out a cigarette, put it into the angle of his mouth and lit it with a Bic lighter. He turned and faced me more squarely, inhaled deeply, paused, blew out a thin line of blue smoke, looked me squarely in the eye and then almost in tears continued. *"They all say they love me and want me to 'go home' back to the family where I belong and where I will be happy again. What should I do?"*

Perhaps, he was encouraged by my similar accent which he recognized or my automatic responses as a professional listener, even if we were somewhat out of context. I learned that before coming to Vancouver he was a merchant seaman, and had travelled the countries and oceans of the world before arriving in 1972 where, as fate would have it, he met a woman in a gastown pub who subsequently became his wife and mother of his children. I learned that the marriage had never been satisfactory and his yearning for travel took him away for weeks on end as he toured the province, developing a successful yet rather precarious business network.

This was no ordinary casual conversation, and yet from the start, had followed the path of a conventional, outdoor supportive psychotherapy session with the three basic ingredients of exploration, ventilation and occasional advice unfolding sequentially.

As he continued to ventilate, it became apparent through his sobs that despite his existential dilemma, what he really sought (as is often the case) was not advice or an answer, but simply an uninvolved empathetic listener on whom he could unload his burden of unresolved emotional conflict and loss. The similarity between myself and the cornered wedding guest in Coleridge's "Ancient Mariner" struck me forcibly. At one point, when stressing the well-meaning advice of his sister to return to the coop where he spent his formative years, the tears flowed unashamedly down his bristly, weather beaten cheeks, quite oblivious to the passing of others in this rather public arena.

One of the dangers of travel is its addictive properties. The more one sees, the more one realizes the restrictions and limitations of one's own backyard and becomes aware of the novelties and excitements of lands beyond the horizon. Of course it is not everyone who has this in-built exploratory excitability and inner restlessness, but those who do, sooner or later, are faced with the inevitable decision as to where and when to stop.

The compulsive traveller seems possessed by an unconscious urge to go somewhere else where they may find what they are seeking. Unfortunately, one is never able to identify what the goal really is. Others have postulated that the peripatetic traveller is not actually seeking anything at all, but is wandering in order to move away from others in an attempt to avoid intimacy, responsibility or being discovered to be inferior, inadequate or simply a sham. It is not every stone that wishes to gather moss! Pondering on these matters, Rudyard Kipling commented that when all things were considered, there are only two kinds of people in the world those who stay at home and those who do not!

Bruce Chatwin and other well-known travel writers take the Darwinian view, that in our evolutionary past, we were nomadic by nature and those who drift around the world are simply yielding to these more archaic urges. No doubt there are many global wanderers and stoical "stay at homers" who are blissfully content with their lifestyles and with their social and geographical situations, but as one visits countries belonging to what are sometimes referred to as "the new world" and where migration has recently contributed to the population, the conversation in bars and other social gatherings frequently drifts to existential issues and ambivalence concerning the conflict between the culture of origin and present domicile.

As the shadows across Vancouver Harbour continued to lengthen, I left my distressed fellow traveller who, in the space of 25 minutes, no longer seemed a stranger, but more a kindred spirit. He thanked me for my time, shook my hand and disappeared down the wide white steps where he merged into the busy throng beyond. As I hurried back to the gloomy conference hall, an image of one of Paul Gauguin's more depressing Tahitian paintings, came to mind which somehow encapsulated the feelings of my brief uninvited exchange.

Surrounded by voluptuous, bare-breasted South Sea women and a couple of mangy looking dogs, the artist himself squats dejectedly in the bottom left-hand corner, every gesture and angle of his body showing despair and misery. In small print under his feet are the words *"D'ou venons-nous? Qui sommes-nous et ou allons nous?"*

Human beings have been pondering these questions for a long time and despite explosions in computer technology and information processing, no answer is in sight. My brief encounter outside Vancouver convention centre reminded us not only of our ignorance of the meaning and purpose and of life, but also that psychiatry has no special insights into some of the more profound issues of life and existence.

"You cannot travel the path before you become the path itself." – Buddha

SNAKES AND OTHER WRIGGLY THINGS

Anyone who lives in Australia for even a short while and ventures out of the city into the vast empty spaces or the endless seaside regions will inevitably be startled by the sudden appearance of one of the many varieties of snake, several of which are venomous. Fortunately, like most reptiles, they are shy, reticent creatures, avoiding human contact whenever possible. Occasionally, this is not always possible, and disagreeable confrontations occur, usually when they are least expected.

All cultures have myths about snakes. They may sometimes be characterised as creatures of evil and wickedness or they may be associated with goodness and magical healing. Many medical societies around the world depict snakes entwined around staffs of ancient wise healers, whilst the Old Testament indites the serpent as tempting Adam and Eve to partake of the forbidden fruit which led on to sin and the eternal curse of evil in many Western religions.

Whilst aboriginal people have some of the most profound and colourful myths and stories, not just about snakes but about every creature that inhabits this extraordinary land, the recent European arrivals, being of a more pragmatic nature, have a less complex mythology. Perhaps the commonest and yet quite disturbing tale which I have heard repeated in many reputable bars is that of the large venomous snake which, when lying across the road, will ascend the suspension of a passing vehicle and there remain patiently and wilfully until the unsuspecting passengers alight at the end of their journey only to fall victim to the venomous fatal strike.

Any discussion of snakes will soon focus on the length of the reptile in question, and participants will go to great lengths to impress. On several occasions I have heard how a particular specimen was so long that as it crossed the road its head had already disappeared into the bush long before the tail end had emerged from the undergrowth on the opposite side. Whatever interpretation a particular group places upon the significance of snakes there is no doubt that they have been part of the collective unconscious of the human race for a very long time.

THE DEAD SNAKE: A CAUTIONARY TALE

Way down in the remote, sparsely populated south-west corner of Australia are a strange collection of small mountains. Despite being called the Stirlings, after one of the State's early governors, many of the peaks retain delightful aboriginal names of pre-European invasion times and are a pleasant change from the tedious, flat terrain of the surrounding West Australian farmlands and scattered homesteads.

Talyuberup Peak is described by one of the guides to the Stirling ranges as a 'pocket-sized mountain'. True, it is a fairly easy ascent, and the return journey can be completed in less than three hours. Nevertheless, the scramble around the crumbly, rocky pillars on the route to the summit is no less exciting than if they were at three times the altitude.

It was a dull grey day in early October (the Australian winter) and the summit of Bluff Knoll, the highest of the peaks, was hidden by dense cloud. Talyuberup was cloudless and was the obvious choice for the day. Within an hour we were scrambling up the steep ravine leading to the final stony ridge and the exposed, bare summit beyond. Alas, at the top of the crevasse a curtain of swirling mist descended, enveloping us in a fine, penetrating drizzle. What a disappointment. The panoramic view that was beginning to unfold had vanished and we were denied one of the many splendid vistas of this unique range of mountains.

After a couple of damp, uninspiring minutes we turned to descend. Then I saw it! A few metres from the summit cairn was a small, pale grey snake, motionless on the hard stony ground. It lay limp, seemingly inert and bereft of life. Ignoring the advice that I was aware of from countless experts I lost my presence of mind. Transfixed by this damp specimen of creation and seeking confirmation of its mortality I stooped down, picked up a marble-sized rock and gently aimed it at the moribund reptile. My accuracy surprised me as it caught the end of its tail. Despite this insult the grey form made no movement so with infantile courage I prodded it gently with a small stick conveniently lying by my leather boot. It rolled over flaccidly, showing no evidence whatsoever of that mysterious phenomenon we refer to as consciousness.

Disappointed I threw away the wooden life detector and gazed at the swirling mist and towards my wife standing by a small cairn of stones, fastening the cords on her Goretex jacket. A few seconds later I sauntered across the track to join her. It was on the third step that the previously inert life form raised its thin, whip-like head and neck, hissed, and in a flash lunged, sinking its needle-sharp fangs into the soft leather of my walking boot.

DAVE AND THE SNAKE

Life is more fragile than we care to recognise, but occasionally an unexpected event reminds us of the ever present shadow and of the delicate balance between life and death as the following harrowing tale demonstrates.

Dave parked the shiny red twin-cam SRX Yamaha motor bike under the shade of a leafy peppermint tree. After removing the key from the dual ignition and locking system, he extracted an ice cold can from the insulated container behind the shining leather seat and sauntered down to the grassy bank near the the old Guildford railway bridge, spanning the slowly moving grey waters of the River Swan.

It was late afternoon on a warm West Australian summers day and the cooling westerly breeze had already commenced. He was at peace with the world, as he peeled of the the black leather jacket and tossed it on to the ground as a temporary seat, from where he could view the circling seagulls and a solitary pelican glide gracefully across the the water. Following the familiar click there was a refreshing hiss as the aluminium seal was broken and he raised the cold can to his lips. The afternoon had passed pleasantly with his mates, watching the cricket on channel ten sharing a couple of cones. Tonight he was taking his girlfriend to the cinema but right now there was an hour to spare before leaving for home. He felt the cold beer trickle down his insides magically reaching the correct spot somewhere in the depths of his stomach.

Suddenly, without warning the bliss and tranquillity was shattered. As he was balancing the the can of precious liquid on the ground to his right, there was a flash in the grass followed by a sudden stabbing pain on the back of his wrist. Uttering a string of expletives, he leaped to his feet and saw the cause of his distress. There, slithering away into a clump of dry undergrowth was a green snake, its glistening scales reflecting the sunlight as it darted with a feint rustle into a parched tusk of grass.

In a crisis the mind is capable of accelerating to an extent that many thoughts and memories intrude simultaneously. Instantaneously he became aware of sensations of fear, revenge and horror but the over whelming impulse was that driven by the memory of Mrs Green, his old primary school teacher who years ago had taught the class that if they were ever bitten by a snake there were two vital things to do: go as quickly as possible to the nearest casualty department and second make sure that you take the snake with you so the doctor would be able to recognize it!

To his left he noticed an old petrol can which he thought would help his plight and then scrabbled blindly at at the dry grass where the wretched serpent had fled. He felt the instant satisfaction of catching the slimy, twisting tail and pulled it towards him, surprised at the resistance it offered. He leaped to the old can and attempted to introduce the writhing body into the 2 inch diameter hole but unfortunately the beast had different intentions and was gyrating as he attempted to swing the head in the desired direction. He tried to grasp it behind the thin cranium, but caught it several centimetres lower down. Hissing and twisting with with gaping fangs and a twitching forked tongue, it turned and bit him again on the other forearm and then a third time, just below his elbow.

Incensed, furious and bellowing with rage he finally managed to grab it by the neck and stuff it through the dark hole into the black void inside. His time perception had expanded, for what seemed like minutes had taken less than twenty seconds from the first strike to stuffing an oily rag from his tool box into the hole before fastening the can onto his rear carrier with an elastic strap. As he adjusted the hooks he noted the delicate puncture wounds on his forearms and saw the fine trickle of blood oozing out from where the needle sharp fangs had injected their unknown venom.

The inflictions were now beginning to sting and throb and as he turned the throttle control he saw that each bite consisted of two small points surrounded by a larger circle of pale blanched skin. He pressed the electrical starter and the big engine roared into life. He guessed that there were only minutes before the effect of the venom on his system would commence but just what the effects might be was a mystery but he new from folk lore something sinister was likely to occur soon.

As the large Yamaha sped down the highway, he was possessed by panic and despair. He must get to the hospital as soon as possible. Weaving in and out of traffic on the three lane highway, overtaking everything in sight he sped past the casino entrance, swerving in front of a bus and into the left lane of traffic, which turned right under the Canning highway and across the Causeway bridge and into the city and the hospital beyond. As he hurtled between the lanes of traffic towards the right turn the light turned to amber and then to red. Screeching to a halt he became aware of a dull ache in his head and a vague feeling of dizziness, as if his rear wheel had developed a slight wobble. Losing his presence of mind he jumped the light and pointed his bike towards to the city beyond and accelerated, ignoring the chorus of angry hooters and disapproving gestures .

Dave could feel the sweat running down the inside of the helmet onto his neck. His vision was increasingly misty and blurred. He tore round the the large traffic island by the central police station and roared along Wellington Street, oblivious of all, regardless of their size or direction of travel. Fortunately it was rush hour and most of the traffic was travelling in the opposite direction. He knew exactly where the accident and emergency department was as a few months earlier he had taken his young brother after he had fallen from his skateboard and recalled dimly that the road into which he turned was part of a one way system. Now, befuddled and and in a swoon, he was vaguely aware of the second chorus of angry hooters as he wobbled precariously up the hill and into Victoria Square where the short line of taxi drivers shouted abuse as he tottered and weaved the moterbike through their ranks. Finally he pulled up outside the glass-doored entrance directly in front of an ambulance delivering an old man in a wheel chair. With his remaining strength he wrenched the rusty drum off the carrier whilst an exasperated and irate ambulance woman remonstrated in loud expletives. Dave stood glassy eyed for a few seconds before her, visibly swaying as he struggled to maintain his balance. He pulled off the shiny black helmet and attempted to look the woman in the eye but his gaze failed. Just before falling to the ground, he was able to utter a few slurred yet unmistakable words "bitten by a snake mate! it's in the bloody can."

Minutes later an unconscious Dave was carried into the Royal Perth Hospital on a stretcher. Almost immediately he was intubated and admitted to the intensive care department where he remained for several days on an artificial life support system. We can only guess what happened to the snake or whether any one in the casualty department had the courage to open and inspect it evil contents. Sadly, what Dave did not know, was that Mrs Green was correct in 1980 in advising her students how to deal with snake bites, but that in 1999 these precautions are no longer necessary, as modern snake anti-venom contains antidotes to all known species of poisonous reptiles which might possibly inflict their bites on the unwary citizen. Sometimes the hazards of not keeping abreast of recent advances may be catastrophic, but the real problem is not not knowing but in not knowing which knowledge might one day be useful, valid or even essential to life.

TRAIN TRAVEL: THE OLD AND THE NEW

Travelling by train (when one has the time) may not always be the most convenient mode of transport but, in many ways, it is pleasurably unique.

Lal (who runs the local Indian take-away) was quite emphatic when I asked his advice on the best way to cross southern India. As he encased our vegetarian curry and popadoms in a brown paper bag and plastic container, he paused for a few seconds and looked at me seriously; "There is only one way to cross India and that is by train". He was absolutely right and, without hesitation, I would forward the same advice. However, the potential Indian train traveller should know beforehand that there are some idiosyncrasies in the system which will require patience, time and forbearance, as some of-the most simple procedures are both elaborate and paradoxical.

The ticket office is a long, bare room with approximately twenty small guichets, each having a glass window perforated by a small hole through which one shouts one's requests to the Indian Railways official who can be seen dimly beyond. In front of each window is a queue of about thirty people who seem to represent a complete cross-section of Indian society, age and costume. A couple of thin, stray dogs wander about, and an emaciated beggar clad in a dirty loin-cloth sits almost motionless at the back, head bowed and hand stretched out in a gesture of supplication. A dry wind blows the dust and waste paper around the entrance to the hall and a group of small boys chase one another noisily and randomly amongst the general melee. There is a sense of order, but only just!

133

THE TICKET

After preliminary enquiries, we join the first queue apprehensively and learn that this is the line for obtaining a ticket application form. We shuffle forward a few inches at a time, slowly approaching the small hole in the glass window behind which we can see a turbaned official. Small boys carrying straw baskets containing delicious hot, curried Indian delicacies tempt us with their wares. But we are deterred by the rather unsavoury way he handles them with obviously filthy fingers which we imagine crawl with millions of bacteria to which we have, as yet, no acquired immunity.

Soon we can see the man behind the window. He has a small collection of differently coloured application forms and a large old-fashioned, hard-backed ledger into which he meticulously writes down the name, address and nationality of the potential traveller. Having completed this clerical task, he almost reluctantly hands over the precious forms. The time for this procedure takes about twenty-five minutes and we feel quite encouraged. Next, following further enquiry, we join the ticket registration queue (Guichet No.4) which is somewhat longer and moves more slowly than the previous line. As we creep slowly towards the window, we fill in the given forms, using the lonely planet guide as a firm surface to write upon. Name, age, address, nationality of parents, mother's maiden name, number of dependant children are just some of the preliminary questions before enquiries are made about class of ticket, sleeper, place of departure and arrival, etc. More small boys with more appetising savouries tempt us yet again. After thirty minutes we reach the slot in the glass and hand in the completed form. This time, it is a diminutive bespectacled lady, wearing a purple sari and a large vermilion 'third eye' in the centre of her forehead. She scrutinises the form carefully and then, somewhat alarmingly, disappears. A couple of minutes later, returns with a large green ledger, opens it in the middle and carefully copies down all the information from our forms with a large, shiny red and yellow ball-point pen. She then addresses us in a regional Indian accent, to which we respond with gestures of bewilderment. Fortunately, she knows some English and after a couple of corrections, adjusts the carbon paper and writes on an official pink form which she then tears off and hands to us through the glass hole; she instructs us to Guiche ' No.7.

Despite the heat and increasing sensations of thirst and hunger, we trudge optimistically to the third and final line of assorted travelling companions. By now, the queues are longer, there is a higher level of chaos and we are pleased to have made an early start to the day. Finally, after another thirty-five minutes of standing, shuffling, changing feet and sweating, we reach the actual ticket dispenser himself. He takes the pink form and makes a hand-written record of it in yet another large ledger, then asks us for the fare. Having already calculated the amount, we hand over a wad of grubby paper rupees and wait nervously; he counts it carefully before it putting it in a wooden drawer to his left; he adjusts the carbon paper and neatly writes out a receipt which he passes through the hole. Next, comes a 'sleeper authorisation slip' and, finally, the two cardboard tickets on which are actually printed the details and time of the train.

We experience a sense of victory and achievement as there are terrible stories of people queuing all day to obtain an Indian railway ticket, so we feel pleased as we walk out of the booking hall and into the heat and perpetual chaos of Hydrabad streets. We are pleased, as from beginning to end we succeeded in obtaining our ticket in about two-and-a-half hours. We carefully file our tickets, sleep vouchers and receipts into the depths of our document wallets for safe-keeping as we do not require them for another couple of weeks.

THE JOURNEY

We arrive at Quillon railway station in good time as we have heard frightening stories about unpunctual trains and over-booked compartments. We need not have worried. The train is already waiting in the station, as are hundreds of noisy, excited people. Once again, the crowd is a complete cross-section of dress, colour, religion and age. People are carrying large, battered suitcases, large and small cardboard boxes, plastic carrier bags or small hessian sacks. Many women balance their possessions on their heads, seemingly oblivious of their presence. The scene is different in all respects to the glum, grey crowds who wait at St Pancras for the next train north.

We find the station master's office, submit our sleeper authorisation slips and are courteously handed our sleeping packs which are all neatly labelled and are waiting for us. Each consists of small hessian satchels containing a sheet, a blanket, a piece of soap and small towel. The station master's assistant is a thin, angular, bald man who speaks good, clear English. He instructs us where to find our carriage and wishes us a pleasant voyage. So far, so good.

There are three classes of travel on Indian railways. First class is quite luxurious, with upholstered seats and air conditioning; second class contains firm, yet quite comfortable seats but without air conditioning; third class is definitely quite basic, with wooden seating and no glass in the windows, resembling more the inside of a truck, rather than a railway compartment. Whole families crowd into these bare compartments and sometimes overflow into the corridors where more people sit on boxes and cases, or even lie on the floor, apparently oblivious to the dirty feet of fellow passengers.

The train journey from Kerala across India is not just fascinating, it is a unique cultural experience. After leaving the luscious tropical plains, two enormous diesel locomotives haul the long line of old wooden coaches slowly and majestically through the densely forested Ghat Mountains. The line twists and snakes slowly upwards, sometimes across old stone viaducts and through short, dark tunnels. The whole construction is a supreme example of railway engineering and a credit to the engineers and workmen who laboured in the last century contributing to its construction. Nearly always is the presence of people at work – digging, clearing, lifting, carrying, planting or simply gathering produce in the many small plantations that one passes. Occasionally, the traveller sees men and elephants working together as they carry large tree trunks to waiting trucks.

Our second class carriage had no outside doors and, whilst this may appear a little hazardous to the timid, it enables the traveller the opportunity to sit on the step and hang on to the brass handles in the gap. This practice gives the wonderful feeling of being part of the passing scene and not compartmentalised or separate. As the train ascends, the carriage-step sitter can wave at onlookers and feel temporarily part of the landscape itself.

The magic of crossing India by train is not just a territorial experience, it is also a journey through time. This temporal experience is two-fold. First, much of what one observes reflects a pastiche of a civilisation long since gone in one's own country. There are people walking, carrying and working the fields by hand, usually assisted by beasts of burden. Wooden ploughs, scythes, adzes and trenching tools are implements still in daily use. There are few proper roads in this part of India. Instead the countryside is criss-crossed with narrow paths and lanes through fields where people walk to and from their labours and dally activities.

Second, if one commences the journey early in the morning, the traveller experiences in one day, the full spectrum of Indian life as village after village, slowly pass by. The sun rises, people come out of small dwellings and farms; beasts of burden can be seen shackled and prodded into the first activity of the morning and thin wisps of smoke spiral up from hundreds of wood-burning cooking stoves. As the day progresses, groups of chattering, smartly-dressed satchel carrying children, wend their way to the local school.

The train rumbles on and the day becomes progressively warmer – by lunch time it is very hot. The train stops at a small town that is cluttered with electric poles and criss-crossed wires. At the windows, small boys appear with baskets of fruit and mouth-watering rice savouries and strange, fried, crispy delicacies. We are now unable to resist and exchange our money through the window. I get off the train and join a group of people drinking from a very large fountain which Spouts water high into the air. I splash myself with the tepid water and, refreshed, wander along the seething platform. There are people, dogs, cows, chickens and railway officials everywhere; amputees, blind people and beggars, some seemingly malnourished, trying to persuade others to drop a few rupees into their outstretched hands. After about twenty minutes, an imperious-looking guard marches down the platform, waving a large red flag; he reaches the guard's van at the rear of the train and blows his shrill whistle, and we shudder forward once again into the simmering heat beyond. The train gathers momentum, people leap on and off at the last minute, reminding me of childhood trips to the Yorkshire coast on old steam trains.

Soon we level out and begin a slow descent through dense tropical trees. There are many clearings and, again, in places we see men and elephants toiling together moving massive fallen trunks. I sit on the steps where one would expect a door to be, my legs dangling a few feet from the moving ground below, mesmerised by the *clickety-click* of wheels on rails and the ever changing theatre of rural India passing before my eyes as the day slowly unfolds.

Later, the countryside flattens and we traverse large, less densely populated open plains. The sense of timelessness, the lack of clues as to which century we are in, is occasionally broken by the sight of a motor car or tractor, but the most enduring memory, reminding me of modernity, was of three little boys playing cricket on a rough patch of land. With one mighty slog, the red leather ball rocketed across the empty space toward the passing train and as the perspiring fielder/bowler gave chase, he excitedly returned my wave and

I wished that I could dismount and join in the universal game.

And so the journey through a day in India continues until dusk, when the deep red and orange hues of the setting sun filter through the haze and illuminate all with an unreal mixture of crimson light and contrasting black shadow. As we turn on the compartment lights, thousands of others respond in the darkening gloom outside.

The following day we arrive at the seething, bustling, unbelievably crowded city of Madurai in central India. The railway station is a vast old building, and obviously the arrival of trains is a constant source of curiosity and entertainment for there are throngs of people everywhere, most of them seemingly without any major purpose except to be part of the arrival scene. We assemble our packs, consult the map and study our fore-planned itinerary, carefully noting the time three days hence when we are due to depart on the next connection to Madras in the east.

Being forewarned of beggars and pick-pockets, we push our way through the heaving throng of humanity to the large exit ahead, wondering what more unique experiences lie in wait.

As we emerge, blinking in the bright sunlight, we are surprised to hear a cultured Indian voice calling out our name. In disbelief we turn around to see who could possibly be hailing us in this foreign city. To our astonishment, we see a trim, middle-aged Indian immaculately dressed in a white suit, running after us. He is clutching a clipboard file and a length of white paper trails from his pocket. We stop, and after regaining both his breath and composure, he asks if we have enjoyed our journey and then requests, "Please, may I have your names, please?". "Who is this man?", I wonder. "Police, drug-trafficker, carpet salesman, or tourism promoter?", all went through my mind. However, before I can respond, he addresses us again, "You must be Doctor and Mrs Spencer?". "Thank you, yes", I reply in bewilderment. "Thank you, thank you", he responds with great politeness, as he ticks off our names on a list attached to his clipboard file. Then, with an affable smile, he thanks us, turns and disappears into the melee of Madurai railway station. The interchange lasts about thirty seconds but during this time we note from his lapel badge that he is an Indian Railways official and the paper is a streamer-long computer print-out.

We are immediately impressed by the irony and incongruity of this experience. Somehow as a result of the hours of queuing for our railway ticket and the recording of information onto the ancient cardboard ledgers, some of the data has actually been side-tracked into a computer system, transmitted across India and then activated by our arrival. Somehow this double system - this marrying of the ancient and the new, the medieval and the contemporary, is the very essence of the Indian system. Bullock carts standing next to Boeing 747's, nativity scenes by the roadside, cows on the highway and in shop doorways, are all reminiscent of the impression that in India, one foot is still in the Middle Ages whilst the other stands in the twentieth century. There are no greater memories of this paradox than the twin experiences of lodging one's credentials in an ancient ledger file, only to learn later that somehow this has almost magically been converted into the mystery of computerised record-keeping systems. The old and the new continue to function together in unison, but, as yet, there is a reluctance to release for ever the tried and trusted routine of the traditional system which is itself a legacy of the now obsolete colonial era.

HOPE AND SHAME

Hyderabad is a hot, dry, dusty city especially in the middle of February. The whole repertoire of life takes place on the streets and there are people everywhere. Some sit alone, others are in groups talking animatedly amongst themselves whilst others will be sitting, just gazing into space. There are more who are walking purposefully and hurriedly to unknown destinations. Mothers mingle amongst throngs with small babies strapped to their backs. Many of these infants look healthy and well, but others appear thin, cachexic and with running noses, discharging eyes and sticky ears.

Thin men and little boys squat by the roadside selling fruit, clay pots, hardware, cutlery, pharmaceuticals and many other intriguing yet unrecognizable Indian gadgetry. Others sit with an assortment of tyre levers, puncture outfits, wheels and spanners, waiting to help the next unfortunate vehicle traveller who breaks down. It is probably possible to buy all the necessities of life, including shoes, clothes, toiletries and cigarettes without ever going into a shop in Hyderabad.

In addition to the throngs of people, the road also provides territory for dogs, goats, cows and chickens which wander about in a haphazard manner. These beasts are not only tolerated but in no small way are responsible for some of the weaving and swaying and erratic flow of motor vehicles. These consist of a disorderly mixture of trishaws, rickshaws, mopeds, scooters, men-drawn carts, ox-carts and large black cars, 90% of which are instantly recognizable to an Englishman as an old Morris Oxford, long since discontinued in Britain although there is now an importer of these stately machines in London.

The seemingly endless, disorderly collection of internal combustion engine machines and life forms compete with elderly windowless diesel buses, which crawl around the city picking up long lines of patiently queuing people. The combination of noise, smoke, heat, dust and the sheer pressure of population density blend together and evoke in a visitor a compulsive sensation of life and energy, which is paradoxically both repulsive and energizing in an unexplainable way. One is thrown back into medieval times as ancient ox-carts lumber slowly by, grossly overladen with piles of fruit, vegetables or animal fodder. Occasionally coming around a street corner, one is suddenly confronted by a nativity scene, complete with an infant child in a manger and farm animals wandering aimlessly around insearch of a mouthful of hay or a spare carrot. There is also an awareness that this might be the scene in fifty years' time in the western world if the current population explosion continues unabated.

It is not just the constant chaos of life that creates anxiety for the western traveller. There is also a sense of friendliness and familiarity. Perhaps this is because it is only very recent in history that this form of existence was shared by us all but has become lost by the processes and rules of western civilisation. Indian begging is not akin to those pathetic people who sit in shop doorways or the underground stations of London. It is an active, purposefully directed activity in India and one is made to feel pursued, guilty and occasionally shamed.

The victim who is usually a traveller or tourist of some form is first followed through the market or street. Often, one becomes aware of a tapping on the shoulder by a thin, skinny hand, often accompanied by a thin pleading voice, mournfully repeating a request for a small amount of money. Gaze persistence is another most discomforting phenomenon. The visitor usually wishing to just browse and wonder at the vast and fascinating array of goods and produce, notices that several of the seated locals are watching every move that one makes. This is not the glimpse of idle curiosity. It is a fixed, penetrating gaze which evokes a sense of uneasy tension in the recipient. There is no smile, no blinking and no sign of any emotion which might give a clue to the thoughts of the looker. As the visitor nervously shuffles and moves away, one of the onlookers follows. The pursuer is usually lame, disabled or a woman with a thin, frail-looking child on her back with an outstretched hand. By now the visitor, completely over-whelmed by a blend of shame and fear, fumbles in the pocket and hands over a collection of loose coins and escapes into the anonymity of the crowded alley as quickly as possible.

To the visiting doctor, the streets are an ongoing ward round of human sickness, pathology and disability ranging from an assortment of dermatological conditions, neurological disorders, orthopaedic contractions, blindness, paralysis, leprosy, malnutrition, malignancies and an assortment of afflictions defying kerb-side diagnosis and leaving the medically-trained voyeur with a sense of therapeutic despair and bewilderment.

Shortly before lunch time one hot and dusty morning, my wife and I were half-sitting, half-leaning against a low wall on the opposite side of the chaotically busy road leading to the local bus terminus. Across the street, thousands of patiently queuing people jostled for seats and spaces surging forward each time a bus pulled up at the dusty kerb side. Despite the clamour and pushing, there was always a vestige of order and somehow the system seemed to function. In the middle of the road, the spectrum of human activity continued. People peddled randomly on bicycles, mangy dogs loitered, motorized trishaws and scooters hurtled in all directions discharging two-stroke emissions to the already polluted air. Old women spat red betel nut-stained saliva onto the ground and everywhere was alive with the hum and intensity of Indian life.

After a morning of touring local markets, queuing for train tickets and trying to avoid beggars, we were exhausted and thought we had finally found a spot where we were unrecognizable as tourists and were blending imperceptibly into the scenery. No one was staring, no one was begging and it was relaxing and fascinating just to be a neutral part of the general surroundings.

However, it was not to be for long. Fifty metres away on the crest of the hill came a thin, angular man wearing nothing but a filthy, white loin cloth. His head was bare and balding in the centre, but from the sides grew long, white hair which blew about wildly in the hot, dusty Wind. His face was a picture of agony, anguish and despair as he made his way slowly along the road towards us. He travelled painfully and laboriously, not only because he had no legs but his vehicle was an old hessian sack upon which he rested the remnants of his buttocks and leg stumps. As he propelled himself agonisingly forward with his hands upon the ground, he espied us and fixed us in his gaze. His direction changed as he began to track in our direction. When within approximately twenty metres, he began to shout in high-pitched, vibrant tones "Hey! Hey! Hey!" The voice was pleading, yet simultaneously menacing and demanding. His riveting gaze bore right into us with awesome penetration. Soon, we could hear the scratching of the sack on the grimy dirt of the road beneath. We could see the callouses on his knuckles, the fly ridden sores on his leg stumps, and the dirty sweat that trickled down his forehead in the midday sun which in turn was a source of refreshment to the ever-waiting flies. As he drew nearer, an overwhelming sense of panic and flight overwhelmed me. I turned to my wife and shouted "Run! Run!" Grabbing her by the arm, I pulled her across the seething road, dodging a wandering cow and a couple of trishaws, seeking the anonymity in the crowd of waiting bus-passengers. As we ran and staggered across the road, his plaintive cries intensified: "Hey! Hey! Hey!" I sensed the gaze of hundreds of others who were witness to this disgraceful, humiliating and cowardly display.

Neither before nor since have I abandoned the sufferings of another human being in such a blatant manner. How I wished today and everyday that I had placed a few paltry rupees into his outstretched, gnarled hand instead of fleeing for the security of my air-conditioned hotel. The sense of shame lives on and I hope that this poor man who had so little and has obviously suffered so much has forgotten the incident. Like the ancient Mariner's Albatross, the memory of the event will remain in my psyche until the day I leave the world and its catalogue of inequalities and unfairness. I sometimes wonder if he is still alive and if so, whether he has any recall of this unhappy event, for my memory of it will remain until my dying day.

KERALA
Dangers Above and Below

For me, there are few experiences as spectacular and splendid as swimming in the clear, still, watery world surrounding a coral reef. The simple invention of the face mask enables man to enter into the magical environment of the underwater world. The moment one's head dips beneath the surface, there is an instantaneous transformation in both time and consciousness. Here before the eyes, one is confronted with the aquatic origins of life and of forms that existed millions of years before our ancestors crawled out onto the muddy shores. All around are fish of every size, shape and colour imaginable. They swim together in pairs or in large shoals, twisting, turning or just nibbling at shining lumps of pure white coral. All of them seem to be purposefully directed, even intentional in their busy activity. Are they conscious? Do they plan ahead? Are they, as they seem to be, goal-directed? Who knows? The more one reflects on the matter, the more complex become the questions. Perhaps, one should be content to just experience it all in wonderment, mystery and feel grateful, even humble, that we are accepted without protest as we intrude into this archaic ancient world of our marine ancestors.

India is surrounded by warm seas and vast stretches of coral reef with its own variety of marine tropical fish. So my wife and I were easily persuaded by two keen young boys to accompany them in their outrigger canoe to the nearest tropical reef. A fee was agreed upon, and we arranged to meet the following day. At 10.00 a.m, we arrived at the beach. It was a warm humid morning. Large breakers from the Arabian Sea crashed and rolled onto the white sandy shore where several long dug-out canoes sat expectantly. Abdul and Mohan were waiting enthusiastically and had brought with them two masks and snorkels for us as planned. They were clad only in old shorts despite the already penetrating heat from the Indian sun. In true health promotion style, we were already doused in Factor 15 oil, long-sleeved shirts and hats and must have made an interesting contrast as we helped push and direct the primitive craft out through the breaking surf into the calmer water beyond, before scrambling aboard.

The term "canoe" is the least inaccurate description of this vessel as it was constructed from a long slender tree trunk about 4 metres in length and converted to resemble a nautical craft by being hollowed out from prow to stern, presumably by a sharp iron implement such as an axe or adze. Each end had been shaped to make it more boatlike and streamlined, and the whole vessel was stabilized by the attachment of a long bamboo outriggger by two slender poles on the port-side. As we set off through the clear waters of the Arabian sea, it was obvious that the tree-trunk had been selected purely for its buoyancy properties and it is still a mystery as to why it had been hollowed out at all, for the waves simply broke over the sides and filled the sitting compartment. Consequently, passengers were obliged to sit in the lukewarm water like a bath which sloshed about their thighs and buttocks. Our two Indian hosts sat at prow and stern with large wood paddles, being the only source of power driving us away from the town of Kovalam, south to the promised tropical fish. The simple craft made good speed and we chatted cheerfully and amicably in broken English as we proceeded first past palm-fringed shores, then around a small headland on which was built a large vivid pink mosque complete with minarets and a large T.V aerial. We glided by an old rusting Victorian iron pier extending out from an ancient stone harbour wall. Abdul and Mohan became progressively more animated and excited. "Just round the corner, Boss", said Abdul as he increased his stroke, "just round the corner, lots of pretty fish for you to look at!"

By this time, I realized that we were not being taken to a natural coral reef but an artificially created one as occurs when old car bodies and similar junk are thrown into tropical waters. Indeed, in many parts of the world, old tyres and motor vehicles have been strategically placed and within a few years have been overgrown with coral which in turn attracts a whole spectrum of reef fish and marine life in what was previously devoid of aquatic life altogether.

As the two boys negotiated the craft to where I was assured were "lots of fish", I donned the snorkel, moistened the face-mask and prepared to jump in. I observed that we were approximately 30 metres from a harbour wall on one side and about a kilometre away was a straggling village complete with a small harbour, fishing-boats and the usual assortment of people, bicycles, wooden houses, scooters and the faint yet familiar pollution haze that hovers over most of India.

As I sank into the silence of the clear warm waters, I felt a sensation of relief from the scorching heat of the Indian sun, and a sense of expectancy as I entered the underwater world. A small school of brilliant yellow fish swarmed around busily, solemnly observed by a large mournful looking grouper. The bright sunlight illuminated the water and the foundations of the harbour wall. There was a great variety of fish. Two brilliantly-coloured angel fish were busily nibbling at the coral-encrusted ramparts of the pier and a little group of purple gammas fossicked around the remains of an ancient sunken boat. As my eyes adjusted, I was aware of many fish that I had never previously seen and could hear the faint crackle of tiny bubbles rising to the surface as a million tiny creatures respired and exchanged vital gases so necessary to life. It is a shame that there was no true reef, but there was no shortage of tropical fish life, so there was obviously an abundance of nutrient of some sort to sustain them all. I was shortly to discover what.

I came up for air a few metres from the canoe, re-adjusted the face-mask and snorkel before diving down for another period of exploration. As I submerged, I half-noticed another canoe in the direction of the distant village and that an elderly man was perched precariously on the stern. Back in the waters below, I returned to the world of poster coloured fish and sparkling water. Above, I could see the shadow of both our canoe and the other one I had just glimpsed. There was a flurry of excited activity under the latter vessel, and it appeared as if something was attracting them and provoking their interest. I swam nearer to join the jostling crowd of waving fins and beating gills, curious to learn what was the focus of their interest. Suddenly, and with instant horror, it dawned upon me: this happy flock of tropical marine life forms were feeding, not upon "les fruits de la mer", but upon delicacies being dropped to them by the man in the small canoe rocking about in the swell above.

Earlier on our trip, we had noticed that the Indian male has no special need of a toilet and will eliminate the contents of his bowel with only a minimum of privacy.

Favourite places (we observed) were a few metres off a foot path, on beaches, just inside someone's drive or (most disagreeably) at the end of the local bus station behind the waiting coaches early in the morning.

I twisted in the water, veering off at a tangent in the opposite direction before surfacing some distance away from the offending sphincter which was still hanging over the sharpened end of the dug-out canoe, depositing faecal material into the clear water. I swam urgently back to the craft that was to carry us back to Kovalam Beach, acutely conscious of keeping my lips tightly sealed around the snorkel mouthpiece I shot, almost ejected, out of the water with seemingly little effort or difficulty. My wife seemed surprised to see me return so soon, and Mohan and Abdul could not be convinced that I had truly appreciated the beauties of their Indian underwater world in five minutes. My affinity for such delights and the magic of coral reefs remains, but a twinge of apprehension remains whenever there is the presence of any other craft in sight. Beauty and the Beast are like night and day, never far apart.

CRICKET, CRICKET, CRICKET

The game of cricket is in many ways a metaphor for life. We all know what it means to be "stumped "or "caught in the slips" and which of our friends are good at dealing with "fast bowling" or are clever "spin" doctors.

How many of us have occasionally been "hit for six" or simply "run out." The parallels are almost endless.

The cultural richness of the game is also to be found in many different guises, forms and corners of the world, even if the rules are a little bent, the following are an example.

Not Everyone's Game

It was late August in British Columbia and only the highest mountains in the far distance showed remaining traces of snow on their majestic peaks. The sun illuminated the sparkling waters of the bay and high cotton wool clouds scudded across the clear blue skies. Far away to the west, beyond the Vancouver skyline, lay the unmistakable profile of Vancouver island with its jagged peaks and pine forests. I was one of many spectators on the springy turf surrounding the cricket pitch in Stanley Park, enjoying the scene as two local teams struggled for supremacy with bat and ball.

Stanley Park is a large round finger of delightfully forested land projecting out into the bay, providing the citizen with a haven of peace from the busy turmoil of the adjacent city. Here, one can ride, jog, run, saunter or just meditate, unaware of the close proximity of civilisation. However, to the cricketers on this summer afternoon, the splendour and magnificence of the surroundings were not of primary relevance and all attention was focused on the shiny red ball as it left the bowler's fingers and hurtled through the warm air towards the flannelled-man standing at the other end who was clearly having difficulty not only manipulating his bat to intercept the spinning missile, but also in preventing it from demolishing the integrity of the three wooden stumps behind him. Fortunately (for him), the ball was a few millimetres wide of his off-stump and his attempt to hit it failed completely as it shot through to the large red leather gloves of the wicket-keeper standing a few yards behind.

His apprehension and anxiety, already significantly raised,

was further augmented by his failure to make contact, and he furtively pretended to adjust his right batting glove. As those who have played cricket will know, the small cluster of fielders around the batsman sense this increasing tension and will enhance it even further by uttering expressions of despair, disbelief and feigned astonishment. Small groans of disappointment, loud enough only for the terrified batsman's ear are made and similar comments such as "Another coat of paint" are all part of the vicious psychological warfare frequently employed.

As the ball was conveyed back to the bowler, it passed through three or four pairs of fielders' hands on its way. Each one looked at it wisely, gave it a small polish on' his trousers and lobbed it to the next team member. The bowler (already walking back to his mark) caught it with one outstretched hand and turned. The final ploy in tension escalation at this point occurs when the three or four fielders around the cowering batsman shuffle in two or three steps. This menacing manoeuvre, if executed properly, occurs just as the bowler commences his ferocious run and accelerates towards the delivery crease. Such was the critical situation in Stanley Park this fine afternoon and the tension was shared by both spectators and players alike. The atmosphere was electric and as the bowler turned, there was no sound apart from the drone of a distant aeroplane and the thud of his feet on the turf. This was a culture-specific moment peculiar to those who have been reared in certain narrow Anglophile traditions.

Suddenly and unexpectedly, it all went wrong. Like the telephone ringing just before an orgasm. Such had been the focus of attention on ball and bowler, no one had noticed a small group of native Indians deeply engrossed in conversation, slowly sauntering across the green field. There were three or four adults and a couple of small children. They were dressed in old blue denims, jeans, colourful short sleeved shirts, open sandals and around their necks, they wore shining pearl-like necklaces. Their long hair blew attractively in the gusty wind.

Behind, were silhouetted the deep green trees and the backdrop of the mountains of British Columbia, their homeland. Above all, they were oblivious to the ritualised struggle occurring in their very path as they wended their way to the other side of the field. This little group of indigenous people were completely unaware that anything significant outside of themselves was occurring. Presumably, they noted that some European people in white clothes were hanging around but there was no reason to believe that anything significant was happening.

Fortunately, the vigilant umpire complete with a sweater tied around his waist saw them and raised his arm high in the air. Amongst gasps and groans from spectators and fielders, the bowler, already in full flight and poised for a final lethal delivery, managed to hang on to the ball and slither to an ignominious halt half way down the pitch. In a second, the tension had completely disappeared only to be replaced by bewilderment and disbelief. Every fielder to a man turned away from the scene and ambled towards the boundary, eyes raised skywards, muttering silently to himself. The Indians, still unaware of the hallowed ground upon which they had perpetrated, continued their slow amble across the pitch towards an unknown destination.

It is an ill wind that blows no one any good and on this occasion the batsman alone benefited from this cultural transgression. The demoralised fielding team had lost the initiative and the psychological advantage had evaporated. The batsman went on to score another 26 runs before being run out trying to sneak an extra single.

Interestingly, despite the enormity of this cultural clash, it was not just the Indians (or first Nationers as they are now called) who seemed unaware. None of the cricketers uttered an audible word or sound as they turned their faces to the sky above the boundary. Unconsciously (or so it would seem), there was a tacit reciprocal acceptance and tolerance of each other's cultural styles. Perhaps the game of cricket is a more useful ritualised form of behaviour than it would appear to be.

How Hard is a Cricket Ball?

The relationship between culture and choice of national sport is elusive. Presumably geography, climate, national temperament, colonial history and other factors must all be relevant. Child psychiatrists believe that play in infancy is an essential prerequisite for the subsequent mature development of the adult personality, not just in human beings but throughout the mammalian kingdom. Play has also been demonstrated in birds and even some species of fish.

Ethnologists and psychoanalysts insist that play in children and organised sport in adults is not just fun, it also serves a useful species-preserving function. Competitive sport, they say, is ritualised fighting which permits yet limits aggressive behaviour in civilised society. Unfortunately, these views do not help us in understanding why the French would not condescend to play cricket, yet remain a major force in rugby or why the English are never to be seen playing "boule" on the village green.

The visitor to India, Jamaica or Barbados will quickly observe cricket being played in some form or another almost everywhere. Small boys are to be seen walking the streets carrying ancient cricket bats or perhaps twisting and spinning a worn-out cricket ball in their spindly hands. Wickets are painted on doors and walls, and clusters of local lads are observed playing and obeying the rules of cricket in the back streets of Kingston and other centres of population. One could conclude that this passion for the game is a legacy of the British colonial days when it was introduced during the last hundred years. Unfortunately, this hypothesis is weakened, for in the Bahamas to the north of the Caribbean where the British presence was just as pervasive, cricket is played little and anyone interested in the latest test score will find it frustratingly difficult to obtain.

Despite this unexplainable disinterest in cricket in the Bahamas, I do have a vivid cricketing memory. Under the ramparts of Fort Charlotte to the west of Nassau, is one of the Bahamas' few cricket grounds. The crab grass is a broad leaf variety and the underlying ground is unresilient sand and limestone. Frangipani, hibiscus and elegant palm trees circle this small oval and beyond the long on boundary are the crystal clear blue waters and distant surf breaking over the coral fringes of the lagoon. In the Bahamas, cricket is played in the schools a little and there a few district teams. The proximity to the United States has clearly spawned an interest in such American sports as baseball.

It is the police who seem to take the game of cricket most seriously and on Saturdays during the season, the force will be playing one of the other local teams. These matches are entertaining, not just for the exciting and rapid style of play, but also because of a general repartee and verbal banter between players, and players and spectators which go on most of the time. Because of the small size of the oval and the Bahamians' love of action, most of the runs, as I recall, were scored by boundaries. There was fun and laughter in Bahamian cricket. Every two or three overs, spectators will be entertained by glorious high hits for six, always accompanied by jubilant shouts of approval from the vocal local crowd. Bahamian cricket, as I remember it, was one of the most social variants of the game with almost constant interaction between players and spectators being central.

Late one breezy afternoon, the police team were batting and were obviously in command, dominating some rather inferior bowling. The batsman was a large muscular police sergeant named George Rolle. He wore an old style floppy cricketing cap with a large neb pulled down over his forehead. He had been in for over half an hour and by now had eyes described by one of the onlookers "as big as saucers". The last delivery of the over was rather short and a few inches wide of the off stump. George stepped forwards to the pitch of the ball, raised his bat and made a huge swing which lofted it high into the air above and over the heads of all the fielders towards the mid off boundary. Cheering, clapping and shouts of "good old George" broke out around the ground. As the red leather missile approached the palm-fringed boundary line, it became clear to adjacent onlookers that it was dead on line for a solid object that would instantly arrest its progress. The intervening object was the head of a large man walking slowly round the perimeter with a couple of his friends. He was enjoying the afternoon sunshine and the shouts and warning cries made in his direction were all in vain. With a sickening thud, the ball hit him on the back of his head. For a couple of seconds, there was ghastly silence as spectators and players alike stared in horror and anticipation. The silence was then broken by cheers and shouts of delight as the afflicted man stooped down to pick up the ball which by now had dropped onto the crab grass at his feet. He picked it up, looked at it wistfully and threw it underhand back to the nearest fielder.

Anatomists tell us the skullbones of the African are significantly thicker, denser and consequently stronger than his European counterpart. However, the sight of a fast moving cricket ball suddenly crashing into a human skull vault without causing any apparent damage was quite incredible, to put it mildly, and I watched nervously as the man continued his amble round Fort Charlotte, seemingly none the worse from an insult which I am sure would have put most of us into the neurology ward for intensive observation and possible care.

Play On Mate!

Australian culture has embraced cricket with a tenacity and enthusiasm rivalled only by that in the Indian sub-continent and certain parts of the West Indies. Furthermore, it has become so imbued with cricket as a symbol of natural identity that one could be forgiven for acquiring the impression that Australians believe it was invented there.

This belief has resulted in many local cricketing variants which the visiting English person sometimes finds rather brash and not quite proper. A few years ago, Kerry Packer and his colleagues, recognising the importance and significance of cricket, realised that there was probably a lot of money to be made by zapping it up and commercialising the whole proceedings. He was right! Nowadays, more money is made from Australian one-day cricket than any other variant, and the sight of players dressed in gaudy coloured uniforms using a white ball illuminated by brilliant flood lights has become commonplace. The television audience are flooded with lurid advertisements between overs, brainwashing them into what they should think, what they should buy and how to behave. However, it is still basically cricket. But only just!

Fortunately, the fundamentals remain unchanged, and on Saturday mornings, the parks and sports grounds of Australia are full to capacity with training, coaching and practice matches for all age groups. Thousands of young boys act out their Shane Warne and Steve Waugh fantasies, usually shared by the watching zealous parents. Children recognized as having unusual talent are soon spotted and siphoned off into special coaching opportunities. It is unusual to see wickets against the garage doors in Australia!

In Western Australia, the ground is hard due to the presence of underlying compacted sand. The turf that grows in these conditions has to be watered daily and is not the springy, luscious variety that grows in the wetter, cooler temperate climates of England. Consequently, the ball moves fast on the wicket invariably taking the newcomer by surprise.

Over the hill from the Central Police Station in East Perth, is one of the less attractive cricketing ovals of the city. On one side, is the railway line whilst beyond the long end boundary, is an old untidy cemetary. Away in the distance, one can see the long line of low hills which simmer hazily in the heat of summer but assume a dull green hue, during the months of winter rain.

Late one afternoon in early March, the University's second team were engaged in their annual contest with one of the local private schools. The tea interval had finished and play had resumed for about ten minutes. A couple of hundred spectators sat about in folding chairs, on rugs or on blankets. Ice chests and Eskies were everywhere and seemed to contain an inexhaustible supply of cans of beer, bottles of wine and Coke. Most people wore shorts, sunglasses and flannel hats. A couple of barbecues were smoking away, and the invasive smell of beef-burgers and sausages hung about the still warm air.

Despite their seniority, the University were doing badly, and after being all out for less than 200 runs, were having difficulty in dismissing the younger super-keen schoolboy players who had already made 109 for the loss of only 3 wickets. In desperation, the University Captain had decided to engage one of the spin-bowlers to see if he could dislodge one of the more troublesome high-scoring batsmen. The bowler was a black-haired engineering student obviously of Italian or Yugoslav parentage who, like many children, had Central European parents who had never heard of cricket before migrating to Australia, but had now taken the game up with great enthusiasm.

As he turned to commence his short curved run from round the wicket, the umpire, noticing a disturbance from the cemetary boundary area, raised his hand in the air, effectively preventing the delivery of the expected leg break. Just in time! Running across the oval, sweating and breathless, was a rather overweight shabbily dressed Aboriginal man. He was unshaven and his bloodshot eyes fixed on the horizon, betrayed both fear and intention. Seconds later, he crossed the pitch without a side glance and was gone. The bowler returned to his short run mark, and the umpire signified him to recommence. Alas! No sooner had he taken the first measured step when he was once more aborted by the ever-vigilant umpire's arresting signal.

A second Aboriginal man was now approaching the field of play and quickly crossed the centre of the pitch. This man was somewhat older and even larger than the first interloper who was by now disappearing through some scrubby bushes by the railway track. Like his predecessor, he was sweating, breathless and lumbering unsteadily rather than running. Clearly, he was angry and in pursuit of the former. This was apparent, not just from his facial expression, his body language and because he was following the identical path, nor because of the expletives he was uttering but because in his right hand, he was carrying a large broken glass bottle. As he moved across and out of the field of play, there was a mumble, just audible, of low-pitched Australian murmurs, groans of dissent and resigned disapproval from both spectators and players alike.

Seconds later, without any observable display of emotion, the umpire waved his right hand and the long-awaited delivery curled down the wicket only to be blocked by a dead-straight bat. The ball trickled to the silly mid on fielder who picked it up ruefully, rubbed it on his trousers and returned it to the bowler for the next delivery as if nothing unusual had happened. All in a day's play!